T0136405

Security and Resilience of Cyber Physical Systems

This book addresses the various security and privacy issues involved in the cyber physical system (CPS). There is a need to explore the interdisciplinary analysis to ensure the resilience of these systems, including different types of cyber threats to these systems. The book highlights the importance of security in preventing, detecting, characterizing and mitigating different types of cyber threats on CPS. The book offers a simple approach to understand various organized chapters related to the CPS and its security for graduate students, faculty, research scholars, and industry professionals.

The book offers comprehensive coverage of the most essential topics, including:

- Cyber physical systems and industrial internet of things (IIoT)
- Role of internet of things (IoT) and their security issues in cyber physical systems
- Role of big data analytics to develop real-time solutions for CPS
- DDoS attacks and their solutions in CPS
- Emulator Mininet for simulating CPS
- Spark-based DDoS Classification System for cyber physical systems

The book is aimed at undergraduates and graduates studying networking, IoT, and cloud. Healthcare and automobile industry professionals will also find this book useful.

Chapman & Hall/CRC Cyber-Physical Systems

SERIES EDITORS:

Jyotir Moy Chatterjee
Lord Buddha Education Foundation, Kathmandu, Nepal

Vishal Jain
Sharda University, Greater Noida, India

Cyber-Physical Systems: A Comprehensive Guide
By: Nonita Sharma, L K Awasthi, Monika Mangla, K P Sharma, Rohit Kumar

Introduction to the Cyber Ranges
By: Bishwajeet Pandey and Shabeer Ahmad

Security Analytics: A Data Centric Approach to Information Security
By: Mehak Khurana & Shilpa Mahajan

Security and Resilience of Cyber Physical Systems
By: Krishan Kumar, Sunny Behal, Abhinav Bhandari and Sajal Bhatia

For more information on this series please visit: https://www.routledge.com/Chapman-
-HallCRC-Cyber-Physical-Systems/book-series/CHCPS?pd=published,forthcoming&pg=1
&pp=12&so=pub&view=list?pd=published,forthcoming&pg=1&pp=12&so=pub&view=list

Security and Resilience of Cyber Physical Systems

Edited by
Krishan Kumar, Sunny Behal,
Abhinav Bhandari
and Sajal Bhatia

CRC Press
Taylor & Francis Group
Boca Raton London New York

CRC Press is an imprint of the
Taylor & Francis Group, an **informa** business

A CHAPMAN & HALL BOOK

First edition published 2023
by CRC Press
6000 Broken Sound Parkway NW, Suite 300, Boca Raton, FL 33487-2742

and by CRC Press
4 Park Square, Milton Park, Abingdon, Oxon, OX14 4RN

CRC Press is an imprint of Taylor & Francis Group, LLC

ISBN: 9781032028569 (hbk)
ISBN: 9781032028637 (pbk)
ISBN: 9781003185543 (ebk)

DOI: 10.1201/9781003185543

Typeset in Palatino
by Deanta Global Publishing Services, Chennai, India

Contents

Preface

In order to understand what it means, cyber physical system and its related security issues among the research community, students, researchers, and teachers must develop both a foundation of cyber physical system and an understanding of key elements of security issues related to it. This book provides a complete understanding of state-of-the-art work on security issues in cyber physical systems in connection with the internet of things (IoT) and other recent networking technologies such as software-defined networking (SDN), big data, and cloud computing, successfully blending theory and practice. In addition, this book focuses on content related to the security challenges and issues of cyber physical systems, the general workflow of cyber physical systems, the possible vulnerabilities, attack issues, adversaries' characteristics, and context-aware security frameworks for general cyber physical systems, with a special focus on potential research areas and problems in IoT networks.

In addition, this book shall encourage both researchers and practitioners to share and exchange their technical experiences and recent studies between academia and industry to highlight and discuss the recent developments and emerging trends in securing the cyber physical systems and its applications. This book includes nine high-quality chapters from established security research groups, researchers, and prominent academicians worldwide, which address important issues from theoretical and practical aspects.

Editors

Dr. Krishan Kumar earned a B.Tech in Computer Science and Engineering from the National Institute of Technology, Hamirpur, India, in 1995. He earned an M.Tech in Software Systems from BITS, Pilani, India, in 2001 and a Ph.D. from the Department of Electronics and Computer Engineering at the Indian Institute of Technology, Roorkee, in 2008. Currently, he is a Professor in the IT department at UIET, Punjab University, Chandigarh, India. His general research interests are in information security and computer networks. He has published over 200 research papers in different international journals and conferences of repute, including more than 1,500 citations.

Dr. Sunny Behal earned a B.Tech in Computer Science and Engineering from Shaheed Bhagat Singh College of Engineering and Technology, Ferozepur, Punjab, India, in 2002. He earned an M.Tech in Computer Science and Engineering from Guru Nanak Dev Engineering College, Ludhiana, Punjab, India, in 2010 and a Ph.D. from IKG PTU, Kapurthala, India, in 2018. His research interests include Botnets, DDoS attacks, and information and network security. Currently, he is an Associate Professor in the Computer Science and Engineering Department at Shaheed Bhagat Singh State University, Ferozepur, Punjab, India. He has published more than 70 research papers in different international journals and conferences of repute.

Dr. Abhinav Bhandari earned a B.Tech in Computer Science and Engineering from G.T.B.K.I.E.T, Malout, India, in 2001. He earned an M.Tech in Computer Science and Engineering from D.A.V.I.E.T., Jalandhar, India, in 2008 and Ph.D. from Dr. B.R Ambedkar National Institute of Technology, Jalandhar, in 2017. He worked as Head of Department at Lala Lajpat Rai Institute of Engineering and Technology, Moga, India, from 2006 to 2010. He has been an Assistant Professor in the Department of Computer Engineering, Punjabi University, Patiala, India, since

2012. His areas of interest are computer networks and network security. He has guided more than 20 M.Tech students in their dissertation works. He has published more than 50 research papers in reputed journals and national/international conferences. He has acted as a guest editor for a special issue of a Scopus index journal, *Advances in Mathematics: Scientific Journal*, for the International Conference on Applications on AI and Machine Learning ICAML-2020 and ICAML-2021 organized at the Department of CSE, Punjabi University, Patiala, India.

Dr. Sajal Bhatia is Assistant Professor of Cybersecurity and Director of cybersecurity programs within the School of Computer Science and Engineering at Sacred Heart University, Connecticut, USA. His primary research interests revolve around network security, in particular areas such as Denial-of-Service (DoS) attacks, synthetic traffic generation, critical infrastructure security, and intrusion detection. More recently, he has been interested in exploring industrial control system security, cyber physical system security, and cybersecurity education. Dr. Bhatia's teaching interests include network security, intrusion detection, capstone and senior projects, network penetration testing, and computer networks. Prior to joining Sacred Heart in 2017, Dr. Bhatia worked as Postdoctoral Faculty and Visiting Assistant Professor at Fordham University, New York, USA, and as Postdoctoral Research Scholar at Vanderbilt University, Tennessee, USA, where he explored the area of secure and resilient cyber physical systems. He earned his Ph.D. from the Information Security Research Institute at Queensland University of Technology, Brisbane, Australia, in 2013. He earned a B.Tech in Communication and Computer Engineering from the LNM Institute of Information Technology, Jaipur, India, in 2008. Prior to starting his doctoral studies, he worked as Project Associate at IIT Kanpur.

List of Contributors

Name of Author	Affiliation
Naveen Aggarwal	University Institute of Engineering and Technology, Punjab University, Chandigarh, India
Fathi Amsaad	Eastern Michigan University, Ypsilanti, MI, USA
Mohamed Baza	College of Charleston, SC, USA
Abhinav Bhandari	Department of Computer Science and Engineering, Punjabi University, Patiala, India
Vaibhav Chaturvedi	Department of Civil Engineering, Dr. B.R. Ambedkar National Institute of Technology (NIT) Jalandhar, Punjab, India
Amardeep Chopra	Department of Computer Applications, SBS State University, Ferozepur, Punjab, India
Anubhav Dwivedi	Department of Mechanical Engineering, Aarhus University, Nordre Ringgade 1, 8000 Aarhus C, Denmark
Dikchha Dwivedi	Department of Computer Science and Engineering, Rama University Kanpur, India
Chakshu Goel	Department of ECE, SBS State University, Ferozepur, Punjab, India
Amit Grover	Department of ECE, SBS State University, Ferozepur, Punjab, India
Brian Hildebrand	Eastern Michigan University, Ypsilanti, MI, USA
Navjot Jyoti	Research Scholar, SBS State University, Ferozepur, Punjab, India
Karamjeet Kaur	University Institute of Engineering and Technology, Punjab University, Chandigarh, India
Navneet Kaur	Department of Computer Science & Engineering, Dr. B.R. Ambedkar National Institute of Technology (NIT) Jalandhar, Punjab, India
Sukhveer Kaur	University Institute of Engineering and Technology, Punjab University, Chandigarh, India
C. Rama Krishna	Department of Computer Science and Engineering, NITTTR, Chandigarh, India
Krishan Kumar	University Institute of Engineering and Technology, Punjab University, Chandigarh, India

Rajiv Kumar	Department of Civil Engineering, Dr. B.R. Ambedkar National Institute of Technology (NIT) Jalandhar, Punjab, India
Meet Kumari	Department of Electronics and Communication Engineering, Chandigarh University, Mohali, India
Veenu Mangat	University Institute of Engineering and Technology, Punjab University, Chandigarh, India
Mahesh Patel	Department of Civil Engineering, Dr. B.R. Ambedkar National Institute of Technology (NIT) Jalandhar, Punjab, India
Mayank Pathak	Department of Civil Engineering, Dr. B.R. Ambedkar National Institute of Technology (NIT) Jalandhar, Punjab, India
Nilesh Vishwasrao Patil	Department of Computer Science and Engineering, NITTTR, Chandigarh, India
Anuradha Rani	Department of Computer Engineering, SBS State University, Ferozepur, Punjab, India
Abdul Razaque	New York Institute of Technology, New York, USA
Hari Om Sharan	Department of Computer Science and Engineering, Rama University Kanpur, India
Vishal Sharma	Department of ECE, SBS State University, Ferozepur, Punjab, India
Anu Sheetal	Department of Engineering and Technology, Guru Nanak Dev University, Regional Campus, Gurdaspur, India
Gurpreet Singh	Department of Computer Science and Engineering, Punjab Institute of Technology, Rajpura, India
Jagdeep Singh	Research Scholar, SBS State University, Ferozepur, Punjab, India
Mehtab Singh	Department of Electronics and Communication Engineering, Satyam Institute of Engineering and Technology, Amritsar, India
Ravi Pratap Singh	Department of Industrial and Production Engineering, Dr. B.R. Ambedkar National Institute of Technology (NIT) Jalandhar, Punjab, India
Manish Snehi	Department of Computer Science and Engineering, Punjabi University, Patiala, India
Suvidhi	Department of Computer Science and Engineering, Punjab Engineering College (Deemed to be University), Chandigarh, India
Jyoti Verma	Department of Computer Science and Engineering, Punjabi University, Patiala, India

1

The Cyber Physical Systems and Industrial Internet of Things (IIoT): A Revolution

Meet Kumari, Mehtab Singh, Amit Grover,
Anu Sheetal, Chakshu Goel and Suvidhi

CONTENTS

1.1 Introduction

Today, industries are moving from the product-centered to the service-oriented design, with the internet-of-things (IoT), cyber physical systems (CPSs), artificial intelligence (AI), and information technology (IT) driven paradigms. From this point of view, smart manufacturing industries should consider the smart product – service designs that can be seen as the task collaboration through service execution as well as the generation of novel services and co-created values. With the advancement of technologies such as cloud computing, CPSs, big data analysis, industrial IoT, and digital twin, there is a huge possibility to boost the growth of smart CPSs [1]. The CPS is an emerging discipline that involves engineered communication and computing systems interfacing with the real world. The fourth phase, IIoT, is driving the future industrial revolution as it will quicken the industrial journey to a novel transformation of economic level that shall further open growth and competition. The four levels of industrial revolutions are shown in Figure 1.1 [2].

Today, IIoT seems to be enhancing our world through smart connected sensors, automobiles, etc. There were more than 30 billion connected devices around the world by 2021 [2]. The recent literature reviews on the CPS-IIoT systems are given in Table 1.1.

DOI: 10.1201/9781003185543-1

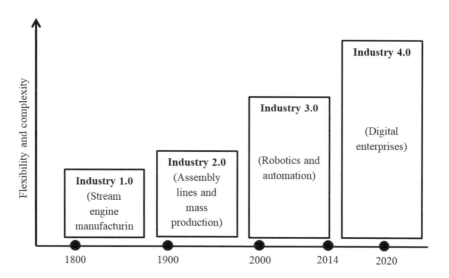

FIGURE 1.1
Industrial revolutions [2].

The main aim of this chapter is to present the IIoT concepts based on CPS security architectures, along with major issues, applications, and future scope.

1.2 CPS-IIoT Architectures

Industrial IoT enfolds industrial devices and systems such as communicated meters, flow gauges, waste water structures, manufacturing robots, and pipeline monitors. For an organization, industrial sectors illustrated in Figure 1.2 are severity relevant and nature of threads. All sectors make maximum use of IIoT based on industry trends through market research companies.

As IoT, a domestic implementation aims at enhancing entertainment and convenience. But the IIoT is an "Industry 4.0", the team created in Germany. In "Industry 4.0", the CPS looks for physical processes by creating a virtual copy of the real world and provides decentralized decisions. Here, the CPS cooperates and communicates with humans and each other in the physical world. Factory control systems' hacking is increasing day by day. The major attacks or security issues are as follows [16]:

a) Understanding the offline to online shift infrastructure
b) Arranging security temporal dimensions
c) Managing the implementation issues for optimum practice
d) Handling the infrastructure complexity

TABLE 1.1

Recent literature reviews on CPS-IIoT systems

Year	Authors	Focus
2012	Bufan Liu et al.	Cost-effective manufacturing procedure recognition method for CPS-enabled shop floor on the basis of deep transfer learning [3]
2017	Pradeeban Kathiravelu et al.	Reducing the challenges of CPS systems with a software-defined method [4]
2018	Yingfeng Zhang et al.	Framework for CPS-IIoT-based smart production logistics systems [5]
2018	Patrick Strauss et al.	Predictive maintenance enabling in the brownfield using low-cost sensors for IIoT-CPS architecture and machine learning [6]
2018	Paula Fraga-Lamas et al.	Implementation and validation of a Bluetooth v5 Fog industrial CPS architecture for IIoT [7]
2019	Bufan Liu et al.	Edge-cloud orchestration operational solution architecture on the basis of CPS and IIoT [8]
2019	Sachin Sen et al.	Security improvement and operational performance approach for big data and IIoT in CPS systems [9]
2019	Anthony Wadsworth et al.	IIoT monitoring and control security development scheme for CPS [10]
2019	Ishwar Singh et al.	IIoT and CPS integration in the learning factory [11]
2019	Michael Nolan et al.	Adaptive IIOT/CPS messaging methods for enhanced edge compute utility [12]
2021	Zhengang Guo et al.	Self-adaptive collaborative control based on CPS for smart production-logistics system [11]
2021	Mian Ahmad Jan et al.	Lightweight mutual privacy-preservation and authentication scheme for intelligent wearable devices in IIoT-CPS [13]
2021	Julio Moreno et al.	Security reference designs for industrial CPS [14]
2021	Shiyan Hu et al.	CPS systems and IIoT based on cloud-edge computing [15]

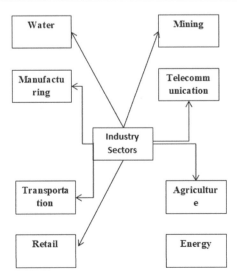

FIGURE 1.2
Industry sector category.

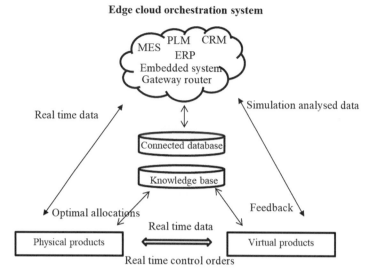

FIGURE 1.3
CPS-based IIoT for smart products [8].

Figure 1.3 presents the CPS-based IIoT architecture.

1.3 Applications

Major applications of CPS-based IIoT architecture are as follows [2]:

1. *Smart Manufacturing*: In IIoT-based industries, the products and machines interact with one another to drive machines and manufacturing materials by communicating with the IIoT-based systems. Factories with raw products and network machines exist today, although these self-contained structures will be interconnected jointly in a comprehensive system where all materials, devices, and machines will be sensor devices that will communicate and connect with each other, also known as the CPS. Industry 4.0 is dependent on the CPS-based IIoT by communicating with and controlling each other. Smart manufacturing enables factory managers to arrange and analyze information automatically to optimize products and make better-informed decisions. In addition, due to the reduction in sensor costs, the application of sensors in industries is rapidly increasing, and advanced analytical application introduction can be utilized to reveal and extract insights from the raw data, as shown in Figure 1.4.

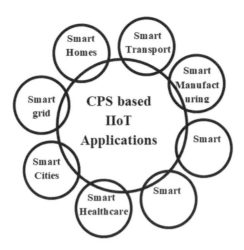

FIGURE 1.4
Major applications of CPS-based IIoT applications [16].

2. *Smart Agriculture*: The world population is going to reach 9.6 billion by 2050. Thus, to sustain this global population, the agriculture industry must encourage IoT. In spite of challenges like severe climate conditions and increasing weather changes and the atmospheric impact of in-depth agriculture practices, the requirement for more food to feed the growing population has to be fulfilled. In IoT-based agriculture, the farmers and producers would be benefitted by minimizing the waste, improve fertilizer utility and increase in productivity. Thus, data are collected using smart farming sensors such as climate conditions, crop's growth process, and soil quality. These data can be utilized to handle the business state, equipment efficiency, staff performance, etc. Further, better internal controlling processes result in lower production risks and, hence, waste reduction and cost management, thanks to the enhanced production control. Automation processes, use of smart devices, pest control, and irrigation provide efficient business to the farmers.

3. *Smart Cities*: The deployment of smart cities is multidimensional. However, in urban centers there are various usage cases, which can vary depending on the city size and the local jurisdictional control. In smart cities, sensors bridge to sense different things such as degradation and seismic force effect at work. In roadways, sensors are used to sense subsidence and traffic flow as well as wear and tear of the roads. Better security, facial recognition within buildings (apartment or commercial) and offices (private or government), and many more can be achieved by CPS-based IIoT deployment.

4. *Smart Home*: Smart home, or home automation, offers home security, convenience, comfort, and energy efficiency by providing control devices, apps, or network devices. A CPS-based IIoT shares smart home devices and systems to operate together, automating actions and sharing consumers' data on homeowners' preferences. In smart homes, using smart garage doors and locks, residents can deny or grant access to visitors. Also, with smart security cameras, homeowners can monitor their homes when they are outside the home. To identify the different types of residences, pets, visitors, burglars, etc., smart motion sensors can be used. Along with sensing electric surge and turning off appliances, household systems can also monitor the freezing pipes and sense water failures.

5. *Smart Healthcare*: Precision medicine to diagnose illness through AI trends in machines defines the associated genomic understanding, treatment plan defining, and success probability prediction of the treatment zooming in appropriate monitoring and treatment operations. For maximum precision, algorithms are trained differently for all diseases and conditions (labor intensive and costly), which has been in the deployment process and not commercialized for the past few years. In everyday life, precision health monitoring means outside treatment every second in outside centers and hospitals.

6. *Smart Transportation*: Travelling to the grocery stores for fresh nutritional supplies every day is a routine in our lives. In smart transportation, automatic vehicles are easily available on roads. There are five systems in smart transportation vehicles that can help connect various IoT and groundwork, laying for full autonomy.

1.4 Challenges

The various CPS-IIoT challenges are as follows [2]:

a) *Security Vulnerabilities*: Continuous disfiguring of high-profile aims keeps this issue regularly in the back of human minds. Changing the disinfectant blend ratio at a water treatment plant to stop the nuclear power plant cooling system could potentially place a city in immediate danger.

b) *Connectivity*: Connecting various devices will be a major challenge in the future CPS–IIoT system and will disobey the architecture of current communication designs and underlying technologies. Presently, the dependency on the centralized, authorized, and authenticated client/server creates the issues.

c) *Legal Issues and Regulatory*: This applies primarily to healthcare devices, insurance, banking, infrastructure, and manufacturing. Today, this consists of various laws such as CFR 21 part 11 and GAMP 5. This further adds to the cost and time needed to bring the products into the market.

d) *Network Determinism*: This is essential for almost all CPS-IIoT-based areas such as security, control applications, transport, communications, manufacturing, and healthcare devices. The usability of the cloud currently inflicts a 200-ms delay, which is acceptable for some applications, but not for security-related applications, which require a fast response.

e) *Lack of Standardization and Architecture*: Regular fragmentation in CPS-IIoT implementation will degrade the values and enhances the end users' costs. Some reasons for these fragmentations are privacy and security fears, market dominance jostling, avoiding intellectual property issues with competitors, and lack of clear leadership.

f) *Scalability*: This is not much of a major issue, but it is sufficient to become a primary issue in relation to the consumer cloud due to the increase in the number of operation devices. It causes enhancement in the bandwidth and time to verify transactions.

g) *Sensor's Limitations*: Various sensors such as light, sound, color, laser scanner, radar, and motion are performing well for IIoT applications. In addition, current advances in solid-state sensors and microelectronics will make the sensors less challenging in the presence of noise and complexity in the coming future.

h) *Durable and Dense Off-Grid Power Sources*: While Wi-Fi, 4G, etc. are capable of solving major connectivity challenges, some shortcomings of battery life exist in the system. Besides these, more security challenges are given in Table 1.2.

1.5 CPS-IIoT Future

The IIoT future has a limitless ability, as shown in Figure 1.5. The rise in IIoT will bring the future factory 4.0 to reality. Advancements to the IIoT will be promoted through enhanced network agility, AI, and the potential to deploy, secure, and automate diverse applications at hyper scale. An emerging future IIoT wave applications will bring to human life is the interactivity between machine and human and vice versa, where human 4.0 will provide humans to communicate in real time over large distances [2].

This will offer novel opportunities in remote surgery, learning, and repair. After mobile, immersive mixed applications have the ability to become the

TABLE 1.2

CPS-IIoT security challenges [16]

Security challenges	Applications				
	Smart grids	Transportation	e-health	Manufacturing	Smart cities
Mobility	Low ●	High ●●●	Medium ●●	Low ●	Low ●
QoS constraints	Medium ●●	High ●●●	Medium ●●	Low ●	Low ●
Lack of standardization	Medium ●●	Medium ●●	Medium ●●	Low ●	Low ●
Safety	Medium ●●	High ●●●	Medium ●●	Low ●	Low ●
Attacks	Low ●	High ●●●	Low ●	Low ●	Low ●
Resource constraints	Low ●	-	High ●●●	Low ●	Low ●
Scalability	High ●●●	High ●●●	Medium ●●	-	-
Heterogeneity	Medium ●●	Medium ●●	Medium ●●	Low ●	Low ●

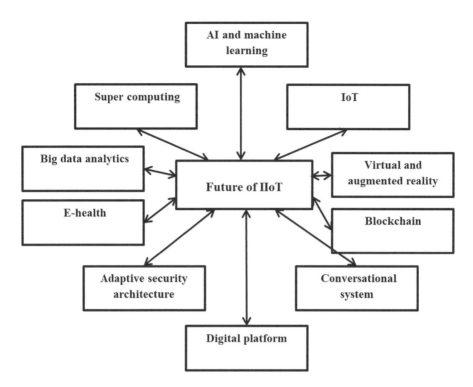

FIGURE 1.5
Future scope of CPS-based IIoT [10].

next platform, realized by haptic sensations and 3D audio, which are becoming our major interface to the physical world. Bringing future IIoT to life will need close interaction between IoT and network platforms. An IIoT solution hugely enhances efficiency, connectivity, time saving, scalability, and cost-effectiveness industrially. It will combine systems and people on the plant floor at the enterprise level, which will provide the organization the main value from their systems except constrained by economic and technological limitations. Due to these reasons, ignition provides the ideal platform for IIoT power bringing into enterprise. IIoT will drastically modify the future of industry systems from wrist watches to smart devices; we have already seen this industry trend come to reality. This will give people the opportunity to have a better standard of living and careers due to the full potential of vision that will lead to unlimited value-creation opportunities. The great potential of IIoT will lead to smart healthcare, power grids, logistics, diagnostics, etc. In the future, IIoT will improve production levels and become the driving force for different types of innovations, along with self-healing, self-configuration, and self-monitoring [10].

1.6 Conclusion

In this chapter, the influence of integrated IoT and the CPS in IIoT on industrial 4.0 has been presented. It is concluded that in spite of having various issues in the CPS, it is most suitable in the manufacturing systems with security, confidentiality, and reliability of users' data. Also, the CPS in IIoT offers various future potential applications such as smart manufacturing, smart agriculture, smart cities, smart home, smart healthcare, and smart transportation.

References

1. Zhengang Guo, Yingfeng Zhang, Xibin Zhao, X.S.: CPS-based self-adaptive collaborative control for smart production-logistics systems. *IEEE Trans. Cybern.* 51, 188–198, 2021.
2. Chanchal Dey, S.K. Sen: Industrial 4.0: Industrial internet of things (IIOT). *Indus. Autom. Technol.*, 269–310, 2020.
3. Bufan Liu, Yingfeng Zhang, Jingxiang Lv, Arfan Majeed, Chun-Hsien Chen, D.Z.: A cost-effective manufacturing process recognition approach based on deep transfer learning for CPS enabled shop-floor. *Robot. Comput. Integr. Manuf.* 70, 2021.
4. Pradeeban Kathiravelu, L.V.: SD-CPS: Taming the challenges of cyber-physical systems with a software-defined approach. In: 2017 Fourth International Conference on Software Defined Systems (SDS), 2017.
5. Yingfeng Zhang, Zhengang Guo, Jingxiang Lv, Y.L.: A framework for smart production-logistics systems based on CPS and industrial IoT. *IEEE Trans. Ind. Inf.* 14, 4019–4032, 2018.
6. Patrick Strauss, Markus Schmitz, Rene Wostmann, J.D.: Enabling of predictive maintenance in the brownfield through low-cost sensors, an IIoT-architecture and machine learning. In: IEEE International Conference on Big Data (Big Data), 2018.
7. Paula Fraga-Lamas, Peio Lopez-Iturri, Mikel Celaya-Echarri, Oscar Blanco-Novoa, Leyre Azpilicueta, Jose Varela-Barbeito, Francisco Falcone, T.M.F.-C.: Design and empirical validation of a Bluetooth 5 fog computing based industrial CPS architecture for intelligent industry 4.0 shipyard workshops. *IEEE Access.* 8, 45496–45511, 2018.
8. Bufan Liu, Yingfeng Zhang, Geng Zhang, P.Z.: Edge-cloud orchestration driven industrial smart product-service systems solution design based on CPS and IIoT. *Adv. Eng. Informatics.* 42, 100-984, 2019.
9. Sachin Sen, C.J.: Operational performance and security improvement approach for integrated bigdata and industrial IoT in cyber-physical communication systems. In: 2019 International Conference on High Performance Big Data and Intelligent Systems (HPBD&IS), 2019.

10. Anthony Wadsworth, Mohammed I. Thanoon, Charles McCurry, S.Z.S.: Development of IIoT monitoring and control security scheme for cyber physical systems. In: 2019 SoutheastCon, 2019.

11. Ishwar Singh, Dan Centea, M.E.: IoT, IIoT and CybeIoT, IIoT and cyber-physical systems integration in the SEPT learning factory-physical. *Procedia Manuf.* 31, 116–122, 2019.

12. Michael Nolan, Michael J. McGrath, Marcin Spoczynski, D.H.: Adaptive industrial IoT/CPS messaging strategies for improved edge compute utility. *Proc. Work. Fog Comput. IoT*, 16–20, 2019.

13. Mian Ahmad Jan, Fazlullah Khan, Rahim Khan, Spyridon Mastorakis, Varun G. Menon, Mamoun Alazab, P.W.: Lightweight mutual authentication and privacy-preservation scheme for intelligent wearable devices in industrial-CPS. *IEEE Trans. Ind. Inf.* 17, 5829–5839, 2021.

14. Julio Moreno, David G. Rosado, Luis E. Sánchez, Manuel A. Serrano, E.F.-M.: Security reference architecture for cyber-physical systems (CPS). *JUCS: J. Univers. Comput. Sci.* 27, 609–634, 2021.

15. Shiyan Hu, Yang Shi, Armando Colombo, Stamatis Karnouskos, X.L.: Cloud-edge computing for cyber-physical systems and internet-of-things. *IEEE Trans. Ind. Inf.* 17(11), 7802–7805, 2021.

16. L Maximilian, Markl E, M.A.: Cybersecurity management for (industrial) internet of things–challenges and opportunities. *J. Inf. Technol. Softw. Eng.* 8(5), 1–9, 2018.

2

Role of Internet of Things and their security issues in Cyber Physical Systems

Amardeep Chopra, Vishal Sharma and Anuradha Rani

CONTENTS

2.1 Introduction

The role of IoT and cyber physical systems (CPS) in several domains, like industry, healthcare, transportation, smart cities, smart grids, etc., is continuously increasing day by day. IoT provides technological integration of physical components in CPS. CPS is collection of devices of physical domain, like controllers, computing devices and physical environment, and is integrated with cyber domain. These devices interact with each other, share information and communicate control commands. Data from physical domain are collected, and after analyzing these data control commands are issued to physical devices via actuators. With the increase of computing devices in the physical system, it is very complex to integrate these devices with humans. Here, IoT plays a significant role in handling such a complex integration through the availability of these devices over the internet. This ability of IoT has revolutionized many domain applications like smart grids, smart transportation, smart grid, smart cities, smart healthcare, etc.

DOI: 10.1201/9781003185543-2

IoT and CPS have a layered architecture [1] where in the first layer all the devices of the physical system are connected at edge nodes. Above this layer is the network layer that is used to provide communication among the devices. Third layer lies in between network layer and application layer. In the application layer, there are various IoT-based applications, as shown in Figure 2.1.

Showing layered architecture of IoT and CPS

The following are some of this chapter's contributions:

- An organized review of the literature on IoT and CPS security challenges
- In the domain of IoT security, identify several strategies and suggestion
- In the case of smart grid and healthcare, identify security issues and requirements.

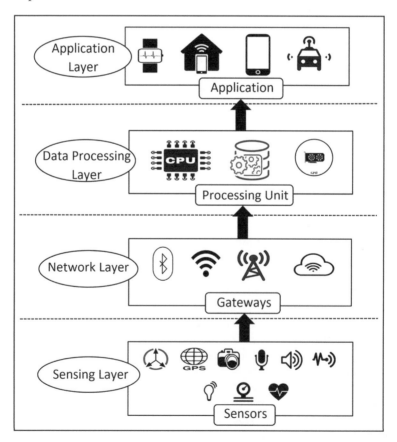

FIGURE 2.1
Showing layered architecture of IoT and CPS. Source research gate.

2.2 Background

There are various challenges to manage these IoT applications due to the following reasons.

- It is a big challenge to handle large volume of data generated by the physical components. The International Data Corporation (IDC) predicts that by 2025 there will be 55.7 billion connected devices on the planet, with 75% of them connected to an IoT platform. According to IDC, data created by linked IoT devices will reach 73.1 ZB by 2025, up from 18.3 ZB in 2019.
- The interaction between IoT devices and humans is complex and is more vulnerable to various security threats. On May 7, 2021, Colonial Pipeline Company, which carries nearly 45% of the gasoline and diesel consumed on the east coast of the United States, was forced to shut down operations due to a cyberattack. The firm that owns the pipeline has reportedly paid a ransom of $5 million to the cybercriminal gang that launched the hack after a ransomware attack on a vital US pipeline network caused a disruption in fuel deliveries in the eastern United States. According to various news reports, the payment was made with Bitcoins.

So, security measures are required at every stage of data acquisition, data communication, control signal processing and also at interlayer communication. Also, with the increase of connected devices and [2] energy constraints of backup devices, it requires some energy-efficient adaptive algorithm to handle unforeseen attacks.

2.3 Security attacks in IoT and CPS

1. Physical layer

   Devices in the physical domain in CPS lie in unsecured environment and are easily [3] vulnerable to physical damage and hacking of controller and actuators in decision process. Also, sensors and actuators are vulnerable to sniffing, spoofing and data leakage attacks.

   The physical layer's key security threats are listed below.
   - Physical destruction [4], tempering and hacking of physical components can lead to system failure or information disclosure and so on.
   - Equipment failure due to aging or environment conditions can lead to abnormal working of the system.

- Failure of power line leads to failure of nodes' working.
- The devices in CPS are installed in unsecure and [5] open environment and any electromagnetic interference can be caused by external electromagnetic signals, which causes a device's, a transmission channel's or a system's performance to deteriorate.
- Denial of service attacks: the attacker consumes network bandwidth. It has the potential to cause the target system to stop functioning.

2. Network layer

Network layer is vulnerable to denial-of-service [6], man-in-middle and information leakage, eavesdropping and IP spoofing security attacks. The network attacks are classified into two types: active attacks and passive attacks. Active attacks alter the data and passive attacks only monitor the network activities. According to Quick Heal report, the following are the detection highlights of different network attacks, as shown in Figure 2.2.

Showing Quick Heal report highlighted network attacks

3. Control layer

Control layer is a very important layer in CPS which is used to control the functionality of physical devices, and any unauthorized access to this layer can impact the overall security and safety of CPS.

FIGURE 2.2
Showing Quick Heal report highlighted network attacks. Source Quick Heal report 2020.

Security attacks in the control layer can disturb the timely action of connected devices and can lead to synchronization problems. In CPS, both data captured from physical world and control signals are most critical and are [7] vulnerable to eavesdropping or information monitoring. Also, the information that can be manipulated by the attackers can lead to all types of attacks, like denial of service, information stealing, replay, etc.

4. Application layer

This layer is the main part of decision making in CPS. Data security and user privacy are the main concern for this layer. In this layer, various services of [8] applications are provided through different protocols. Some applications on the application control layer will acquire a large amount of personal information from users, such as their health status, purchasing patterns and so on. As a result, concerns about privacy must be addressed in CPS. The following are the major security threats to the application control layer.

- Any unauthorized access to user's data can lead to leakage of user privacy. An attacker can misuse these data for further attacks related to financial domains, and issues in data integrity may arise.
- Any [9] Malicious code injected by the attacker can lead to security issues for both the system and the data.
- Any distributed denial of service can lead to interfere, and even block the normal network communications.

2.4 Security measures for CPS

Various types of attacks, like malware, cryptographic attacks [10] and networks attacks on cyber physical system, are a big threat and need some mechanism to implement cybersecurity measures, process, techniques and methods to prevent CPS resources from unauthorized access, data modification, disclosure and destruction. The cybersecurity measures listed below are divided into tiers based on the level of security required. The physical layer of the cyber physical system is primarily concerned with the organization's physical security. Sensors, actuators, RFID devices and image capture are all CPS devices that must be protected. The following are the steps to be taken to design a secure CPS.

- Design should include security constraints.
- Design should be adaptive toward resource efficiency.

- Design should provide secure communication.
- Design should provide data confidentiality.

The physical layer security is concerned with safeguarding equipment such as sensors, actuators, RFID devices and image capture devices, which form the foundation of the CPS. The following are some of the known execution layer's security procedures for perceived security concerns.

- Node authentication policy is needed to protect and secure the nodes in the system. This will lead to the safety and efficiency of the system. So, a more balanced authentication policy needs to be developed to protect the physical devices in CPS.
- A secure user interaction is needed to protect a node's data. For this, biometric access technology can be used to access the physical devices placed in the open field. It is preferable to safeguard node perception data.
- In order to provide authorized access besides the password technology, other technologies, like technology for privacy protection, secure routing and data fusion for safety and secure positioning technology, can be used.

2.5 Cyber security measures for the transmission layer

The transport layer is responsible for providing communication data among the nodes of the system. Security measures are needed to protect the communication data security systems. This layer needs to provide [11] consistency, confidentiality and data integrity. There are two types of encryption techniques available in the data transport layer security mechanism: point-to-point encryption and end-to-end encryption.

- At the time of every communication between nodes, point-to-point encryption techniques assure the confidentiality of the data. However, because each node can obtain unencrypted data, the nodes' reliability needs are higher.
- Hop-by-hop encryption and inter-network authentication are all security measures. The goal of an end-to-end encryption mechanism is to ensure end-to-end data secrecy, and it can give various levels of configurable security policy security. End-to-end encryption, on the other hand, cannot conceal the source or purpose of data. As a result, there are security issues that an attacker could exploit. End-to-end

authentication, key negotiation and key management are some of the security mechanisms.

2.6 Cyber security measures for the application layer

Application layer is responsible and part of the core decision-making along with control layer in CPS. Strong intelligent processing power is needed to process huge amount of data generated at this layer. At the same time, data security and user privacy must be safeguarded. CPS's application control layer security protections work:

- To manage and enhance system access control policy.
- To implement latest methods for user authentication and encryption mechanisms.
- To monitor network activities in order to implement mechanism of network forensics; strengthen network forensics ability.
- To implement valid, unified and efficient security management platform for CPS.

2.7 Smart grids

Electrical energy is critical in industry and plays a significant role in economic growth. Modern IT technologies are now being used to maximize electricity production by taking consumer demands into account across the distribution system. An integrated network or advanced metering infrastructure (AMI) is deployed between the electricity production centers and the end users in the distribution line smart grid. The smart grid is one of the most important areas in IoT since it coordinates electricity generation with end-user demand. In smart grids, security requirements must be considered. The most important requirements in terms of [12] security and privacy are:

- **Confidentiality**: Massive amounts of data are generated by the smart grid, which must be gathered, stored and evaluated. Some of this information will be sensitive, such as personal information about customers and information about the utilities themselves. To prevent unauthorized disclosure of sensitive information, precautions must be taken.

- **Privacy**: The smart grid's provision for bidirectional information flow between the electricity consumer and the utility supplier is one of its most important features. Privacy protection techniques must be employed to secure the privacy of smart grid users in order to protect such sensitive information.
- **Availability**: The smart meters, network infrastructure and control center, which handles user-server requests and control commands, should all be available at all times. Authorized users should not be denied the ability to handle inquiries by unauthorized users.
- **Integrity**: The "smart grid" has various uses as an efficient and intelligent method for managing and monitoring electricity usage. It efficiently assists energy producers and consumers in the estimation and provision of the appropriate amount of electricity at the appropriate time. The most serious vulnerability to a smart grid system may be when attackers manipulate or falsify information. It's possible that the system will break down and collapse. In some circumstances, attackers may purposefully waste system resources, which could have severe consequences.
- **Non-repudiation**: Non-repudiation in smart grid is the ability to prevent a [13] smart meter from denying its participation in an action in which it took part, such as claiming that the energy reports were transmitted on its own.

2.8 Security challenges

1. Smart grid

   There are certain security challenges in smart grids:
   - **Heterogeneity**: In smart grids, there is heterogeneity of communication standards and information system technologies.
   - **Scalability issues**: The ability of a system or network to be easily expanded or modified to meet ever-increasing expanding demand is referred to as scalability. The development of smart grid is expected to be very desirable in accomplishing scalability [14]. The number of smart meters and control centres is increasing at a very fast pace. As a result, security systems have significant scaling issues.
   - **Vulnerabilities to information system technologies**: The conventional electrical power infrastructure is evolving into a smart grid. In a smart grid, the traditional electrical power infrastructure is combined with information and communication

technology (ICT). Such an integration empowers electrical utility providers and consumers, improves the efficiency and availability of the power system and provides for continuous monitoring, control and management of customer needs. A smart grid is a vast, complex network that connects millions of objects and entities. With such a large network come a slew of security problems and flaws. In this chapter, we highlight the smart grid network's complexity and explain the vulnerabilities that come with such a large, heterogeneous network. The issues of securing the smart grid network are then discussed, as well as how current IT network security solutions are insufficient to safeguard smart grid networks. Finally, we go over the current and future security options for the smart grid. Assaults such as IP spoofing, injection and DoS/DDos attacks are only a few examples.

- **Data sensitivity and privacy**: The AMI is a smart grid component that captures high-frequency energy consumption data in smart grid data management, which often provides rich demographic and lifestyle information about end consumers. The information is frequently shared with a variety of stakeholders. The utility, on the other hand, may not have the users' permission to share potentially sensitive data.

2. Healthcare

As information technology progresses, the concept of smart healthcare has gained acceptance. New-age digital technologies such as artificial intelligence, big data and IoT are used in smart healthcare to transform the healthcare system for all dimensions and make it efficient, convenient and more customized according to the requirement.

2.9 Security requirements

Based on study [15], the following are the security and privacy requirements:

- Authentication: PHRs (Personal Health Record) need to be accessed only through authorized individuals.
- Confidentiality and integrity: In healthcare system, sensitive information related to patient health and personal record is stored. This information is stored in a much-secured manner and suitable policies and guidelines are followed. But this information is vulnerable during exchange of information. So, there should be secured and encrypted communication of this information to implement integrity, privacy and confidentiality.

- Privacy concerns: Patients' personal information should be kept confidential according to their privacy rights. Communication of this information should take place under secure procedures. Besides this, IoT devices' locations and patients' identities need to be hidden.

2.10 Security challenges

There are several security and privacy challenging issues in healthcare applications that need to be overcome. The most important challenges are:

- Resource limitations: Low-speed CPUs are used in health equipment. The central processing unit's (CPU) processing power and speed are less in such devices. Most healthcare devices have low memory. These devices have embedded operating system and complex application software. Their memory is not enough to handle data generated from complex security protocols.
- Mobility: Mostly healthcare devices are connected to internet through IoT and are mobile in nature. These devices are used to measure essential health parameters of a patient and notify the patients' condition to the concerned medical staff.
- Heterogeneity: In healthcare protocols, networks and communication mediums provide connectivity between hospital servers, and sensor nodes are not homogenous and have distinguished security mechanisms. Also, sensor devices used to measure basic vital physical parameters like body temperature, heartbeat, blood pressure, etc. have different unit of measurements. It is very challenging to develop security solution for these heterogeneous devices and environment.

2.11 Conclusion

The IoT is a new technology and it has revolutionized the cyber physical world. The various physical objects are connected through internet and form one unified and intelligent ecosystem. An incipient keenly intellective world is emerging nowadays where humans, keenly intellective-phones, computers and incipient astute objects are connected to the internet. Security of these objects is a concern area nowadays, where latest and modern security techniques need to be incorporated.

References

1. Y. Ashibani, Q. H. Mahmoud. "Cyber physical systems security: analysis, challenges and solutions," *Computers Security*, 2017; 68: 81–97.
2. S. Ali, R. W. Anwar, O. K. Hussain. "Cyber security for cyber physical systems: a trust-based approach," *Journal of Theoretical and Applied Information Technology*, 2015; 71(2): 144–152.
3. C. Konstantinou, M. Maniatakos, F. Saqib, S. Hu, J. Plusquellic, Y. Jin "Cyber-physical systems: a security perspective," in *20th IEEE European Test Symposium (ETS)*, 2015: 1–8.
4. S. Krco, B. Pokric, F. Carrez. Designing IoT architecture(s): a European perspective, IEEE World Forum Internet Things, WF IoT, 2014.
5. J. S. Kumar, D. R. Patel. "A survey on internet of things: security and privacy issues," *International Journal of Computer Application*, 2014; 90(11): 20–6. La HJ, Kim SD. A service-based approach to designing cyber physical systems, 2010.
6. T. Lu B. Xu, X. Guo, L. Zhao, F. Xie. "A new multilevel framework for cyber-physical system security," in *First International Workshop on the Swarm at the Edge of the Cloud*, 2013.
7. L. Zhang, W. A. N. G. Qing, T. I. A. N. Bin. "Security threats and measures for the cyber-physical systems," *Journal of China Universities of Posts and Telecommunications*, 2013; 2020: 25–29.
8. A. Humayed, J. Lin, F. Li, B. Luo. "Cyber-physical systems security: a survey," *IEEE Internet of Things Journal*, 2017; 4(6): 1802–1831.
9. Y. Ashibani, Q. H. Mahmoud. "Cyber-physical systems security: analysis, challenges, and solutions," *Computers & Security*, 2017; 68: 81–97.
10. M. Burhan, A. R. Rana, B. Khan, B. S. Kim, "IoT elements, layered architectures and security issues: a comprehensive survey," in *Sensors*, Multidisciplinary Digital Publishing Institute, 2018.
11. L. Xiao, X. Wan, X. Lu, Y. Zhang, D. Wu. "IoT security techniques based on machine learning-how do IoT devices use AI to enhance security," *IEEE Signal Processing Magazine*, 2018; 35(5): 41–49.
12. F. Dalipi, S. Y. Yayilgan. "Security and privacy considerations for iot application on smart grids: survey and research challenges," in 2016 IEEE 4th International Conference on Future Internet of Things and Cloud Workshops (FiCloudW), 2016.
13. D. Airehrour, J. Gutierrez, S. K. Ray, "Secure routing for internet of things," *Journal of Network and Computer Applications*, 2016.
14. Q. M. Ashraf, M. H. Habaebi, "Autonomic schemes for threat mitigation in Internet of Things," *Journal of Network and Computer Applications*, 2015; 49: 112–127.
15. W. AL-mawee. *Privacy and security issues in iot healthcare applications for the disabled users a survey*. Master's thesis, Western Michigan University, 1903, W Michigan Ave, Kalamazoo, 2012.

3

Secure Blind Signature for Electronic Voting and Electronic Cashing Systems: A Survey

Fathi Amsaad, Brian Hildebrand, Mohamed Baza and Abdul Razaque

CONTENTS

3.1 Introduction

Due to the emergence of technology and its pervasive influence on society, computers have been widely applied to various fields and thereby have played a major role in stimulating the growth of internet technology. For example, computers are applied in politics, military, economics, and education fields. The internet provides an avenue for individuals to obtain the most up-to-date information and continues to change and enhance the fabric of daily life. Such scientific advances have the potential to benefit the personal and professional lives of society's members. Science, however, can be viewed as a double-edged sword. Despite the benefits brought by the internet, security concerns arise that necessitate the development of measures to defend against attacks and flaws inherent in the internet. For example, an attacker could delete, amend, or otherwise tamper with digital transmissions of information over the internet and such attacks could be detrimental to users. Digital signatures [11] were developed to address such concerns by providing methods for authentication and ensuring integrity and nonrepudiation of digital transmissions. Since its introduction by David Chaum [2, 3]

DOI: 10.1201/9781003185543-3

in 1982, blind signature has been applied in a variety of applications, from e-voting to e-cash systems. Among the many digital signature paradigms, blind signature stands out due to its renowned ability to hide signed information. This quality makes blind signature a desirable candidate for uses like electronic voting (e-voting) and electronic cash (e-cash) systems, where there is a need to authenticate user data without letting the signer know anything about the signed data [12]. However, the various parameters and complex algorithms used in blind signature to achieve this quality can lead to an increased computation overhead. Thus, it is necessary to address the trade-offs between blindness and computation speed.

Partially blind signatures. Blind signature suffers from the shortcoming that the signer has control only over attributes bound by the public key [22]. It is not possible for banks to set values for blindly issued coins. Thus, every coin value requires its own unique public key. This introduces the cumbersome requirement that every shop and customer maintain a record of all their public keys. This list is usually stored in a smart card with limited memory and storage capabilities. A handful of e-voting schemes suffer from the same disadvantage. As a general idea, blind signature architecture allows the signer to send a null string of common data with an agreement with the receiver [21, 22].

3.2 Background

3.2.1 Digital Signature Concept

Traditionally, actors in fields such as politics and military enforcement utilized handwritten signatures to sign, for example, diplomatic and business documents. The functions of handwritten signatures are as follows:

- Discrimination: Checking the authenticity of certain documents.
- Unforgeability: No one can forge the signature of the signer.
- Nonrepudiation: The signer cannot deny signing.

The primary rationale behind the functions of handwritten signatures hinges on the fact that every individual has his or her own signature style that is difficult to forge. The uniqueness of an individual's signature provides a means for identifying the signer.

However, it is less practical to use traditional hand signatures in the modern digital age for transactions that require remote or online authentication. The digital signature was developed to address this. Diffie and Hellman [1] define a digital signature that makes use of public-key cryptography.

In general, a digital signature involves the following elements: secret key generation, key and message exchange, and signature verification.

Thus, a digital signature can be viewed as a composition of the quintuple (M, N, K, S, V), where:

1. M is the finite set of possible signature messages.
2. N is the finite set of security parameters.
3. S is the finite set of signature algorithms. For any message m, every $k \in K$, the signature $sig_k(m)$ could be generated by signature algorithm $sig_k(m)$.
4. V is the finite set of verification algorithms. V $(m, k, y, sig_k(m)) \rightarrow \{false, true\}$

Although the functions of the digital signature and the handwritten signature are similar, there are differences between them:

- Handwritten signatures can be imitated. A signature forger can imitate the handwriting of the signer, while a digital signature cannot be imitated.
- Handwritten signatures occur under face-to-face circumstances. In other words, the signer and the receiver sign at the same time and the same place. Digital signatures rely on the internet, so they are independent of face-to-face situations. They are free from the limitations of time and space.

3.2.2 Blind Signature Advantages

Blind signature stands out due to its ability to protect the signed information. Its most notable feature is that it is capable of hiding signed information. The following describes the differences between traditional and blind signatures:

- Handwritten signatures can be imitated. A signature forger can imitate the handwriting of the signer. Being a digital signature, a blind signature cannot be imitated.
- Handwritten signatures occur under face-to-face circumstances. In other words, the signer and the receiver sign at the same time and the same place. Being a digital signature, blind signatures rely on the internet and are independent of face-to-face situations. They are free from the limitations of time and space.
- In addition to the requirements of traditional digital signatures, blind signatures should satisfy the following two conditions:

- The message is invisible to signers. The signer cannot acquire detailed information regarding the message signer will sign.
- The signed message is nontraceable, and the signer should not know the timing stamp of the signed message.

3.2.3 Contemporary Relevance of Blind Signature

As a specific type of digital signature, the blind signature gradually develops under the requirement that a digital signature should be more diverse. For a digital signature to be widely accepted, it should enable the signer to sign the target information without being able to view any segment of that information. Also, the signer is not interested in seeing all the details about the target information. The goal of the signer is to notify others that he has signed.

David Chaum [2, 3] first proposed blind signatures in 1982. After their introduction, blind signatures received a great deal of attention from the information world. As a result, many kinds of blind signatures, such as RSA blind signature, ElGamal signature, and Schnorr signature, were created.

The history of the blind signature can be divided into two stages. During the first stage, which occurred from 1982 to 1996, the main goal of researchers was to develop the strategies of blind signature. Many well-performing algorithms were proposed during this stage. During the second stage, which occurred after 1996, researchers focused on developing blind signature applications for e-commerce and e-government.

The most obvious use case for blind signature is in the signing of testaments. In such a scenario, a testator wants a lawyer to sign the testament to have legal effect, but he does not want to share detailed information about the testament with the lawyer. As a result, a blind signature appears to be an appropriate choice. The two most prevalent applications of blind signature are e-cash and e-voting systems. David Chaum introduced the cryptographic concepts that serve as the foundation for e-cash [2, 9, 10]. In the business arena, e-commerce provides an evolutionary way of trading. Paper trading is inconvenient, especially for block transactions. The development of many internet technologies has also made it possible to generate cash using a blind signature. Consumers can use e-cash to get money from a bank where the bank is not able to trace how the consumer uses it, protecting the privacy of the consumer. Sellers can check the validity of e-cash without getting private information about the consumers. The sellers could get their profit from the bank by withdrawing or transferring accounts.

Election integrity is an essential desideratum for democracy. It can also help enhance voter confidence and accountability. Researchers suggest that e-voting systems are capable of enhancing the security of the voting process and thereby support election integrity [8]. E-voting can also help improve the ease, effectiveness, and efficiency of the election process; improve voting accessibility; and increase election turnout. Another advantage of e-voting is that it does not depend on the geographical proximity of the voters. It enables citizens or soldiers living outside of the country to electronically participate in voting.

Since the introduction of blind signatures by Chaum [2], researchers have proposed a multitude of e-voting schemes based on blind signatures [14–19]. According to [14], a secure e-voting system should meet seven properties:

- Uniqueness: Each voter may only vote once.
- Privacy: Each vote should be kept secret.
- Integrality: Each vote should be secured. No one should be able to change another's vote or imitate another voter.
- Impartiality: No one should be able to obtain the voting results before the ballot is complete.
- Veracity: All votes should be counted.
- Verifiability: Should provide a means for verifying final results.
- Unforgeability: No one except the signer can apply a legible signature to the targeted document.

In e-voting, there are two principles:

- The voter's privacy is protected. In other words, during the voting, others should not be able to trace a voter's information.
- The fairness of voting is guaranteed.

In conclusion, due to the blindness of the blind signature, it can be applied in various fields. With the development of technologies, more and more branches of the blind signature may be developed and such developments will promote more widespread use and applications of the blind signature. Firstly, the blind signature allows owners to make the message invisible. Secondly, the blinded message is signed. Finally, the owners remove the blinding factors and get access to the generated data.

Blind digital signature [7] specifically allows a signer to sign documents under the circumstance that the message owners hide the detailed information of the specific message. Apart from the principles of common digital signatures, the blind signature should satisfy the following two conditions:

- The message is invisible to the signer.
- The message is nontraceable by the signer.

3.3 Properties and Efficiency of Blind Signature

A well-designed blind signature holds the following properties:

- Unforgeability. No one except the signer could apply a legible signature to the targeted document.
- Nonrepudiation. After a signer signs a document, he cannot deny the fact that he signed the document.
- Blindness. Even though the signer signs the document, the detailed information in the document is invisible to him.
- Traceless. Once a signed signature is published, the signer cannot determine the exact time he signed the document.

If a blind signature design satisfies these properties, it can be deemed secure. These four properties are principles in both designing blind signatures and judging the efficiency of the specific blind signature. In addition, a well-designed blind signature takes into consideration operability and efficiency. The following aspects can be used to evaluate operability and efficiency:

- The secret key length
- The length of the blind signature
- The blind signature algorithm and verification

3.4 Applications of Blind Signature in Electronic Cash

E-cash system based on RSA blind signature is put forward by D. Chaum. Despite its simplicity, the system has a profound influence. It is also proved to be effective in the Oracle model [4, 5, 6]. The components of the e-cash system based on RSA blind signature are given as:

Algorithm 10.5: E-cash System Components Based on RSA Blind Signature

1) *Register*
   - Bank chooses large primes p, q and computes $n = p \times q$
   - Bank chooses public key e, satisfying $(e, (p-1) \times (q-1)) = 1$
   - Bank calculates private key d by using Euclidean algorithm extension, which satisfies

$$ed = 1 \bmod \left[(p-1)(q-1) \right] \tag{1}$$

where e and n are public and d is private. The two primes p and q are deconstructed by the bank secretly. $H()$ is a public monomial function.

2) *Withdraw*

After the consumer verifies his identity and claims to withdraw, if the bank is allowed, they perform the following agreement:

- The consumer chooses random x, and then chooses random $r \in Z_n^*$ as a blind factor. Calculating

$$m' = r^e H(x) \bmod n \qquad (2)$$

Send m' to the bank.

- The consumer removes the blind factor:

$$s = s'^{r-1} \bmod n \qquad (3)$$

To achieve the e-cash $\{x, [H(x)]^d\}$.

3) *Payment*

- The consumer sends e-cash $\{x, [H(x)]^d\}$ to the seller.
- The seller verifies:

$$\left\{ \left[H(x) \right]^d \right\}^e = H(x) \bmod n \qquad (4)$$

If the equation is established, the seller sends e-cash $\{x, [H(x)]^d\}$ to the bank. After the bank verifies that the e-cash is untapped, the bank increases the amount of money in the seller's account.

The system is the earliest e-cash system and has a profound influence. However, it has the following drawbacks:

- The cash in the system is nondividable. Once the consumer wants to pay money, he can only pay it in whole, making it inconvenient for making payments.
- The system is a fully online e-cash system. It requires the bank to be connected to transfer the payment.

3.5 Application of Blind Signature in E-Voting

Many e-voting models have been suggested over the years, but the vast majority of them are imperfect. Thus, research in the area of e-voting requires further development. There are many e-voting models, but the following three are the most commonly used:

- Single Election Center. Registration, authentication, and related statistics are completed in a single election center.
- Multiple Election Centers. There are multiple equal election centers. Registration, authentication, and related statistics are completed in multiple centers.
- Candidates as Election Centers. Registration, authentication, and related statistics are completed by protocols between voters and candidates.

Owing to the fact that different election methods have different models, the steps are different. Generally, an election system always has the following steps:

- Registration. During the registration process, a legal voter gets flag information that can be verified later from the election center. The identification and voting information are all included in the flag information.
- Voting. A voter constructs a legal ballot and sends it to the election center via different means.
- Statistics. The election center counts the ballots.
- Verification. For a specific election model, the verification can be determined as individual verifiability and total verifiability. In individual verifiability, the voter believes that his ballots can be taken into election results, while in total verifiability, everyone can verify the authenticity of the election after the results are published.

We take the multiple election centers system as an example. In a multiple election centers system, the voting process can be divided into four parts: registration, voting, statistics, and verification. Assume the voter is U, the registration center is R, the voting department is V, and the voting can be simplified as *Yes* or *No*. Then, the voting process can be described by the following:

1) *Registration*
   - $U \to R$. U verifies his identity and hands in two ballots where a vote can be either a *Yes* or *No*. Each ballot is inputted into the system using a random unique sequence number. The ballots are blinded.
   - $R \to U$. R verifies the identity of U and makes sure that U has not voted. If U is testified, R will return the signature of two ballots to U. Otherwise, R will reject U's request.

2) *Voting*
- Statistics. *V* counts ballots and publishes the results with their sequence numbers.
- *U*. Get two legal ballots after removing blind factors.
- $U \to V$. *U* hands in a ballot to *V* with his decision and encrypts it with *V*'s public key.
- $V \to U$. *V* testifies the signature after decrypting it with the private key. If the signature is valid, *V* checks in the database to determine if there are messages that match the sequence number. If another is found that matches, *V* regards the ballot as repeated and the protocol stops. Otherwise, the sequence number is recorded.

3) *Verification*. The voter testifies whether his ballot is included in the election. Blind signature ensures that the contents of ballots are secret. During registration and voting, both *R* and *V* separately check their database to make sure only people with authentication can be involved in the election process. One can vote only once. During the counting process, the ballot contents are listed by sequence numbers. If a voter fails to find his sequence number or finds the contents changed, the voter has a reason to believe fraud has occurred. Therefore, the protocol satisfies the basic request of e-voting. Currently, most e-voting systems take advantage of blind signature to protect the legitimated rights and interests of voters. Research in e-voting still needs further improvements, and developing a more efficient e-voting system requires further development.

3.6 Conclusion

We introduced the concept of digital signatures and compared them with handwritten signatures. We also discussed the background, development, and contemporary relevance of the blind signature. Since blindness is needed in more and more fields, especially in commerce and election, a blind signature is designed mainly for the encryption of inside contents. The blind signature has four main properties: unforgeability, nonrepudiation, blindness, and traceless. A blind signature that satisfies all these properties is deemed secure. Furthermore, we introduced four established blind signature algorithms in detail: RSA, ElGamal, Okamoto-Schnorr, and DSA blind signature. We analyzed them in three parts: system parameters, signing, and verification. We also discussed and analyzed the merits and shortcomings of each. We discussed the most prevalent uses for blind signature: e-cash and e-voting. For e-cash, two e-cash systems are established: one based on RSA signature and one based on Schnorr signature. We also introduced four processes: register, withdraw, payment, and deposit. E-cash systems based on Schnorr are considered the most efficient e-cash system, due to nontraceability, security, and nondouble spending. We also analyzed the disadvantages. E-voting has three primary election models: single election center, multiple election centers, and candidates as election centers. Then we presented an example based on the multiple election centers model. Many new algorithms for blind signatures are being created. Since research on blind signatures is still developing, developers put more efforts into applications of blind signatures. However, during the application period, many problems may arise. The debugging process helps the perfection of blind signature theoretically.

References

1. W. Diffie and M. Hellman, "New Directions in Cryptography", in *IEEE Transactions on Information Theory*, vol. 22, no. 6, pp. 644–654, 1976, doi: 10.1109/TIT.1976.1055638.
2. D. Chaum, "Blind Signature for Untraceable Payments", in *Advances in Cryptology*, pp. 199–203, Springer, 1983, doi: 10.1007/978-1-4757-0602-4_18.
3. D. Chaum, A. Fiat, and M. Naor, "Untraceable Electronic Cash", in *Advances in Cryptology*, pp. 319–327, Springer, 1990, doi: 10.1007/0-387-34799-2_25.
4. T. Okamoto and K. Ohta, "Universal Electronic Cash", in *Advances in Cryptology*, pp. 324–337, Springer, 1992, doi: 10.1007/3-540-46766-1_27.
5. D. Fang, N. Wang, and C. Liu, "An Enhanced RSA-Based Partially Blind Signature", in 2010 International Conference on Computer and Communication Technologies in Agriculture Engineering, pp. 565–567, 2010, doi: 10.1109/CCTAE.2010.5544900.
6. G. Wang, I. Ray, D. Feng and M. Rajarajan, *Cyberspace Safety and Security - 5th International Symposium, CSS 2013*, Springer, 2013, doi: 10.1007/978-3-319-03584-0.
7. C. H. Duo, Y. Yue, and C. P. Yuan, "The Application of Blind Signature Based on RSA Algorithm", in *Applied Mechanics and Materials*, vol. 241–244, pp. 2290–2294, Trans Tech Publications, 2012, doi: 10.4028/www.scientific.net/amm.241-244.2290.
8. S. T. Ali and J. Murray, "An Overview of End-to-End Verifiable Voting Systems", in *Real-World Electronic Voting: Design, Analysis and Deployment*, pp. 173–217, 2016, http://arxiv.org/abs/1605.08554.
9. D. Chaum, "Security Without Identification: Transaction Systems to Make Big Brother Obsolete", in *Communications of the ACM*, vol. 28, no. 10, pp. 1030–1044, 1985, doi: 10.1145/4372.4373.
10. D. Chaum, "Privacy Protected Payments: Unconditional Payer and/or Payee Untraceability", in *Smart Card 2000*, pp. 69–93, 1989.
11. R. Rivest, A. Shamir, and L. Adleman, "A Method for Obtaining Digital Signatures and Public-Key Cryptosystems", in *Communications of the ACM*, vol. 21, no. 2, pp. 120–126, 1978, doi: 10.1145/359340.359342.

12. S. Brands, "Untraceable Off-line Cash in Wallet with Observers", in *Advances in Cryptology*, pp. 302–318, Springer, 1994, doi: 10.1007/3-540-48329-2_26.
13. C. P. Schnorr, "Efficient Identification and Signatures for Smart Cards", in *Advances in Cryptology*, pp. 239–252, Springer, 1990, doi: 10.1007/0-387-34805-0_22.
14. A. Fujioka, T. Okamoto, and K. Ohta. "A Practical Secret Voting Scheme for Large Scale Elections", in *Advances in Cryptology*, vol. 718, pp. 244–251, Springer, 1992, doi: 10.1007/3-540-57220-1_66.
15. T. Okamoto, "An Electronic Voting Scheme", in *Advanced IT Tools: IFIP World Conference on IT Tools*, pp. 21–30, Springer, 1996, doi: 10.1007/978-0-387-34979-4_3.
16. T. Okamoto, "Receipt-Free Electronic Voting Schemes for Large Scale Elections", in *Security Protocols*, pp. 25–35, Springer, 1998, doi: 10.1007/BFb0028157.
17. M. Ohkubo, F. Miura, M. Abe, A. Fujioka, and T. Okamoto, "An Improvement on a Practical Secret Voting Scheme", in *Information Security*, pp. 225–234, Springer, 1999, doi: 10.1007/3-540-47790-X_19.
18. T. ElGamal, "A Public Key Cryptosystem and a Signature Scheme Based on Discrete Logarithms", in *Advances in Cryptology*, pp. 10–18, Springer, 1985, doi: 10.1007/3-540-39568-7_2.
19. E. Mohammed, A. E. Emarah, and K. El-Shennawy, "A Blind Signature Scheme Based on ElGamal Signature", in *Information Systems for Enhanced Public Safety and Security*, pp. 51–53, IEEE, 2000, doi: 10.1109/EURCOM.2000.874771.
20. T. Okamoto, "Provably Secure and Practical Identification Schemes and Corresponding Signature Schemes", in *Advances in Cryptology*, pp. 31–53, Springer, 1993, doi: 10.1007/3-540-48071-4_3.
21. J. L. Camenisch, J. M. Piveteau, and M. A. Stadler, "Blind Signatures Based on the Discrete Logarithm Problem", in *Advances in Cryptology*, pp. 428–432, Springer, 1995, doi: 10.1007/BFb0053458.
22. T. Okamoto, "Efficient Blind and Partially Blind Signatures Without Random Oracles", in *Theory of Cryptography*, pp. 80–99, Springer, 2006, doi: 10.1007/11681878_5, https://link.springer.com/content/pdf/10.1007/11681878, https://eprint.iacr.org/2006/102.pdf.

4

Investigating Convergence of Cyber Physical Systems and Big Data Analytics to Develop Real-Time Defense Solution

Manish Snehi

CONTENTS

The development of cyber physical systems (CPSs) on a temporospatial scale will revolutionize our world by providing intelligent and novel services and applications across a wide range of domains. The cyber physical system embraces the internet of things (IoT), high-volume heterogeneous data from geographically distributed sources, and integration of the cloud services. The rapid and substantial transformation of CPSs affects many facets of people's lives. It offers a medley of services and applications, such as e-Health, intelligent homes, and e-Commerce. Interconnecting the virtual and physical spheres, on the other hand, introduces new security threats. As a result, CPS security has sparked the interest of both researchers and enterprises. The enormous data from globally disparate intelligent devices exacerbate

DOI: 10.1201/9781003185543-4

the problem, entailing security solutions to process the humongous data in real time. The incorporation of big data analytics into CPS defense solutions poses myriad opportunities to increase resource efficiency. This chapter outlines current solutions, data generations, aggregation, storage, and real-time big data processing tools in the context of cyber physical systems. This chapter has also emphasized that horizontal resource scaling on top of vertical scaling allows cost-effective solutions. Furthermore, we have evaluated the available security solutions and concluded with the recommendation of big data analytics for real-time processing of the high-volume network traffic. We have conducted this research to draw the researchers' attention to the crucial intersection of cyber physical systems, big data analytics, and autonomous intelligent defense solutions to get the best out of the trio integration.

4.1 Introduction

Cyber physical systems (CPSs) are diverse and complicated systems made up of tightly coupled cyber components, physical processes, networking, and computation. Several devices with sensing, processing, and communication capabilities carry out physical operations. Computer systems have become more portable, compact, and capable of communicating with the outside world. Furthermore, CPS components may be interconnected via the internet, enabling system monitoring and management with efficient working and reaction in real time.

4.1.1 Cyber Physical System Workflow

CPSs provide a linked environment with the interconnection of thousands of devices, making management and control more convenient. CPSs evolved through several phases prior to its current form, including intelligent, embedded, and networked systems. An effective threat assessment is a critical component of any CPS security solution. A general workflow of CPSs can be categorized into four main steps, presented in Figure 4.1. CPS's primary role is to monitor physical processes and the environment. It is also utilized to provide feedback on any previous actions performed by the CPS in order to guarantee proper operations in the future [4, 8]. The physical procedure is designed to meet the CPS's initial physical aim. Networking stage deals with data aggregation and dissemination. In CPSs, there may be more than one sensor. These sensors may create data in real time, and several sensors can provide large amounts of data that must be pooled or distributed for further processing by analyzers. At the same time, many apps must engage with networking communication. The computing phase involves reasoning

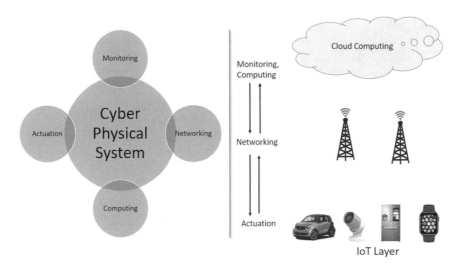

FIGURE 4.1
Workflow for cyber physical system.

and evaluating data gathered during monitoring to determine if the physical process meets certain pre-defined criteria. If the requirements are not met, remedial measures are recommended to be taken to ensure that the criteria are met. The actuation stage carries out the activities that were determined during the computation phase. Actuation can be used to trigger a variety of responses, such as modifying the CPS's online behavior or altering the physical process [20].

4.1.2 Cyber Physical System Architecture

The CPS functions primarily on three levels: perception, network, and application. Each of these tiers is defined by the devices contained inside it and the associated operations that must be implemented. The perception or sensor layer is the initial layer. This layer contains a variety of terminal devices. At this layer, devices can collect real-time data for multiple objectives, analyze information from the sensor's environment, and perform actions from the higher layers [10]. The data communication tier is responsible for bytes exchange and processing between the devices and the applications. This layer's role involves data routing and transmission across different devices and hubs on the networks in use. The third tier is the application tier. Its objective is to analyze the data at the transmission phase and generate commands that control the operation of physical components. This tier performs sophisticated decision-making algorithms on gathered data and critically reflects and provides control instructions for remedial actions. The data communication tier is responsible for bytes exchange and processing between the devices and the applications. This layer's goal is to build a smart environment by

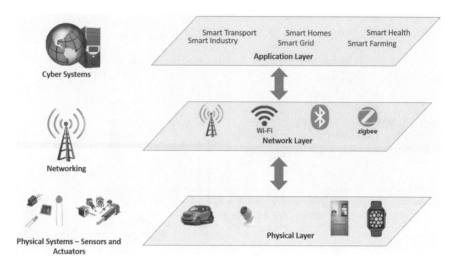

FIGURE 4.2
Architecture of cyber physical system.

combining CPSs with professional industry applications. Figure 4.2 shows the architecture of CPSs.

4.2 Background - Attacks and Security Solutions in CPSs

Attacks against CPSs have the potential to cause substantial physical harm to the surroundings. Each tier of the CPS is subject to passive or disruptive attacks. The CPS is open to network-based attacks [18]. Attacks on nodes, such as the physical devices and components, are examples of perception-layer attacks. Similarly, attacks at the communication layer include data leakage or manipulation of the message and security issues during data transfer. Application-layer attacks entail unauthorized access, resulting in the loss of user privacy. As a result, analyzing possible risks and creating a robust security architecture are required [9]. Each of the CPS layers is vulnerable to common attacks that can be categorized in the following section.

4.2.1 Perception-Layer Attacks

The perception layer is made up of IoT and embedded devices that are confined by limited computer resources and memory capacities and are placed in exterior and outdoor locations, resulting in physical attacks. As a result, those terminal devices are the most vulnerable to a range of attacks. Node capture, fake node, node outage, path-based DOS, and other similar attacks are examples of perception-layer attacks [11, 14].

4.2.2 Network-Layer Attacks

This interface is prone to data theft attacks that occur during data transfer. These attacks capture transmitted messages through a radio interface, alter and retransmit them, or exchange data between diverse networks while imitating the original user. Routing attacks, wormholes, jamming, and selective forwarding are all examples of frequent transmission layer attacks [7, 14].

4.2.3 Application-Layer Attacks

As the application layer collects a significant volume of user data, attacks result in data and privacy loss and unauthorized device access. Common risks at the application tier include user privacy compromise, unauthorized access, ill-disposed code, database fabrication, and administration command imitation. Buffer overflow and malicious-code attacks are common types of attacks at this layer [19, 15].

In cyber physical systems, security is a key consideration. CPSs are often used to monitor and control critically important processes due to their integration with the physical environment, various abilities, and lack of isolation. As a result, any flaw in the CPS's security might have far-reaching consequences. In addition, because they are mission critical, they are more vulnerable to targeted assaults. Many of the primary security needs of CPSs are illustrated by the workflow and the aforementioned CPS features, which any security architecture for CPSs should be built to meet:

1. *Sensing Security:* Because CPSs are inextricably linked to the containing physical environment, the validity and precision of the sensing process must be verified. Sensing security requires physical stimulus authentication mechanisms so that any data captured from a physical entity may be trusted [3, 16].

2. *Storage Security:* After the collection and analysis of data, it may be necessary to preserve it for future use. Any manipulation of the saved data may result in issues in data processing requirements at a later stage. Storage security entails creating solutions to protect collected data in CPSs from physical and cyber manipulation [15].

3. *Communication Security:* The fact that CPSs are networked is a significant feature. This enables them to establish a data integration and transmission network for storage enterprises and coordinate response tasks. Protocols for protecting both inter/intra CPS data transfer from the potential attackers are required for communication security.

4. *Actuation Control Security*: This relates to guaranteeing that no actuation occurs during the passively active phase of operation without the proper authorization. Because the needs of CPSs change over time, authorization specifications must be dynamic.

5. *Feedback Security:* This refers to securing the intermediate systems in a CPS responsible for giving feedback to the physical system.

4.3 Literature Review of Security Solutions in CPS

Any CPS security model should contain defensive security layers. The defensive layer includes features such as brutal penetration, strong authentication, access control mechanisms, a fast reaction time, flexibility to enhancements, and attack mitigation capabilities. Security is a significant concern in cyber physical systems. They are often utilized for controlling and operating mission-critical applications due to their environmental integration, varied capabilities, and lack of privacy. As a result, any vulnerability in the CPS's security might have far-reaching implications. Furthermore, because they are mission-critical, they are more vulnerable to targeted attacks.

Anees Ara et al. highlighted various threats and attacks. The authors also listed defense obligations and tools that apply to CPSs at different layers. They proposed the conceptual models of security that can be adapted into a tiered application architecture [1].

Somali Chatterjee et al. outlined three prominent application engines that have the potential to establish the groundwork for modern technology. Digital agriculture, digital grids, omnipresent IoT, and the medical CPS are all suitable systems (IoMT). In comparison, IoMT presents a distinct set of concerns, including particular crucial safety needs for persons in medical situations [6].

Raj Chaganti et al. demonstrated a customizable device network layer architecture capable of defending against threats and monitoring networks in heterogeneous CPS applications. They discussed the existing challenges with industrial control systems (ICSs), emphasizing the critical nature of an advanced network layer for CPSs [5].

Zhenhua Wang et al. reviewed and analyzed CPS trends in security technologies in three-dimensional space: architecture, application, and MADC (**M**easure of configuration drawbacks, detection of botnets, New **A**ttacks generation for efficient defense solution, **D**evelopment of **D**efense solutions, and **C**ontrolling the attack scenarios), and performed a statistical analysis of article publication time, institute, author, and countries [19].

Yosef Ashibani et al. emphasized the necessary processes to protect CPSs. Their article examines the security challenges at the various layers of CPS architecture, as well as risk evaluation and CPS security strategies. Finally, problems, prospective study topics, and potential solutions are given and debated [2].

Rachad Atat et al. gave the CPS classification by offering a general highlight of data gathering, storage, access, processing, and analysis. They gave a high-level overview of the various security options for CPS large data backup, retrieval, and analytics. They also talk about big data and related challenges in the context of CPSs [2].

Jay Lee et al. discussed the drifts of industrial transmutation in the big data ecosystem and the aptness of predictive informatics means to handle big data to deliver clarity and productivity [9].

Verma et al. has collated benchmark data sets representing the various attack scenarios. The data sets include DDoS, IoT-based DDoS, and other significant attacks [17].

Table 4.1 discusses security attacks at various layers of the CPS and its security management mechanisms.

TABLE 4.1

Security attacks/threats, security requirements, and management mechanisms for CPS

Layers	Attacks/threats	Prerequisites for security	Mechanisms for cyber defense
Application layer	DoS and DDoS attacks, scripting attacks (XSS), SQL injections, buffer overflow, Hijacking of accession, insufficient security configurations, URL access restriction failure	Authentication, key management and agreement, safeguarding privacy, security training and control	Access management, security, and privacy administration
Network layer	Eavesdropping, data manipulation, identity fabrication, IP address spoofing, brute-force password at tacks, denial attacks, man- in-the-middle attacks, key compromise, and packet Sniffing attacks	AAA (authenticate, authorize, accounting), DDoS mitigation, packet encryption, transport layer security	Confidentiality, encryption, data reliability, AAA (authenticate, authorize, accounting)
Perception layer	DDoS due to congestion, physical attacks, interference, exploitation, device dysfunction	Encryption, key management and control	Intrusion detection and mitigation, data encryption, security key management and control, AAA (authenticate, authorize, accounting), securing routing

4.4 Big Data Analytics and CPS Security

The close connection among physical items that gather and send a significant volume of data puts security risks in the limelight in the CPS domain. Data mining is the process of obtaining this relevant information. Before applying data mining to the data, certain processing stages must be accomplished, such as key feature selection, pre-processing, and data transformation. Dimensionality reduction is one potential approach for reducing the amount of data characteristics.

4.4.1 Big Data Technologies

There are several big data tools available for research:

1. Hadoop helps in storing and processing high-volume data.
2. Apache Spark performs in-memory calculation for fast processing and low latency.
3. Apache Storm helps in the faster processing of unbounded data.
4. Apache Cassandra provides highly available and scalable solutions for faster storage and retrieval.
5. MongoDB provides cross-platform capabilities.

Hence, there are diverse and specialized functions that every big data tool performs.

Apache Spark extends the MapReduce model with data sharing abstraction called Resilient Distributed using this extension [12].

4.4.2 CPS Data Mining

The fundamental processes of data mining are divided into three categories: data scanning, rule building, and rule updating. The operator selects the required data through data scanning. Rule construction entails developing candidate rules through the use of selection and development. The administrator verifies appropriate rules before assessing them to determine which ones will be kept for succeeding iterations. The scan, develop, and update cycle continues until the finish criteria. Different prospecting techniques, including cluster, group, and frequent pattern, can make CPSs intelligent.

Clustering enhances the performance of the CPS infrastructure and services of recognition, monitoring, and automation by allowing nodes to share information to determine if they may be clustered together based on the demands of the CPS applications. Classification, also known as unsupervised learning, does not require previous information to complete the splitting of objects into clusters. The goal of frequent pattern mining is to discover intriguing patterns [2].

4.4.3 Big Data Analytics Model for CPS

For various reasons, integrating privacy and security features in business intelligence has attracted the research community's attention. Data are increasingly likely to be kept, processed, and analyzed in several cloud centers, posing security concerns due to the data's dispersed position. Big data analytics handles sensitive data in real time as it treats conventional data, with little regard for security precautions such as encryption or blind processing. Big data stored in physical locations must be protected against ill-disposed trials to defend the processed results.

1. *Source Data Layer*: The source data layer is responsible for gathering raw data from the CPS's physical system's distributed digital sensors. Sources of ingress data include industrial data, the internet, and social platforms.

2. *Intelligent Data Warehouse Layer*: The intelligent data repository layer is a compilation of theories and strategies that support enterprises in controlling and conserving traditional data. It provides a setting in which users may retrieve critical information for analysis.

3. *Smart Data Mining Layer:* This module may condense the data space to a set of most likely states of the study items. The retrieved columns can automatically recognize sets of potential patterns based on the model's inputs. The difference between the actual and inferred states can represent the training model's accuracy. The training data set is used to make the temporal inference. The model precision may be used to select the optimal analytic mining model. Under stochastic working conditions, the data mining model may be used for various mining assignments like regression, categorization, prediction, etc. [2].

4. *Intelligent Data Visualization Layer*: The intelligent data visualization tier can allow stakeholders to get inside details of the modeled data. Visualization methods are used to present the analytic findings on the platform [2].

A reactive feedback system at the publishers and proactive feedforward methods at the subscribers are integrated to increase the quality of real-time data dissemination and achieve resilience. Before being examined by big data analysis technologies like Hadoop, real-time stream data is first transformed into structured form data. Data visualization may be achieved by arranging the data in a representational way. Visualization can also aid in the prediction of real-time cyberattacks. Big data analytics models for CPSs handle large amounts of raw data in order to make better and faster choices in a short period of time.

4.4.4. Horizontal Resource Scaling on Top of Vertical Scaling

Scaling horizontally and vertically are similar in that they both need the addition of computer resources to your infrastructure. In terms of implementation and performance, there are significant variations between the two. Horizontal scaling necessitates splitting a sequential piece of logic into smaller pieces so that it may be processed in parallel across several machines, which is one of the key distinctions between the two. Vertical scaling is simpler in many ways since the reasoning does not need to change.

There are several things to consider when deciding whether to scale out or scale up. Scaling out allows you to combine the power of several computers into a single virtual machine with all of their combined power. Building an application as a single big unit makes it more difficult to add or alter specific bits of code without crashing the entire system. Horizontal scaling provides built-in redundancy as opposed to vertical scaling, which has just one system and hence a single point of failure. As more big multi-core computers become available at much-reduced prices, examine whether your application can be productively packaged in a single box while still meeting your performance and scalability requirements. This might result in cost savings [6, 3].

4.5 Challenges and Future Recommendations

While continuing research focuses on CPS evolution and applications, productive ways to mitigate security vulnerabilities have gotten little attention. The preservation of privacy is a crucial feature of analyzing and mining big data. Future solutions should be based on the hierarchy aspect of various CPS big data applications. The developed solutions analyze the appropriateness of different types of massive data and their performance assessment. Big data analytics is highly recommended in CPS implementation for real-time processing of the high-volume network traffic. The current security solutions are largely focused on data safety. However, it is critical to investigate their effects on prediction and driving algorithms to provide a comprehensive defense against cyber physical security challenges. There are numerous problems with securing CPSs because of their monitoring and actuation characteristics. The following are some of the critical concerns that must be addressed:

1. *The conventional security models* for computing systems have only included cyber threats. However, because CPSs are environmentally associated, interfering with the physical systems around CPSs may result in their failure to work properly. As a result, attackers do not need to tamper with the ecosystem itself but just with the

sensing devices, which may lead the CPS and its security equipment to malfunction [13].

2. *Traditional security solutions* are supposed to fulfill system-wide criteria such as confidentiality, integrity, and availability. These are not static needs, and many more may be required depending on the application. Each CPS function has its own set of security needs, such as sensing, networking, storage, and feedback.

Because many CPS applications are systems of everyday use controlled by nontechnical individuals, security solutions for CPSs should be very usable. We recommend big data analytics for real-time analysis of high-volume network traffic.

4.6 Conclusion

We performed this study to draw the interest of researchers to the critical confluence of cyber physical systems, big data analytics, and autonomous intelligent defensive technologies in order to maximize the benefits of the trio integration. The cyber physical system incorporates the internet of things, large amounts of heterogeneous data from geographically dispersed sources, and cloud service integration. The inclusion of big data analytics into CPS defence systems opens up a plethora of options for resource optimization. We analyzed the current security solutions and found that big data analytics should be used for real-time processing of high-volume network traffic.

Bibliography

1. Anees Ara, Mznah Al-Rodhaan, Yuan Tian, and Abdullah Al-Dhelaan. A secure service provisioning framework for cyber physical cloud computing systems. *arXiv preprint arXiv:1611.00374*, 2015.
2. Rachad Atat, Lingjia Liu, Jinsong Wu, Guangyu Li, Chunxuan Ye, and Yi Yang. Big data meet cyber-physical systems: A panoramic survey. *IEEE Access*, 6:73603–73636, 2018.
3. Aniruddha Bhattacharjya, Xiaofeng Zhong, Jing Wang, and Xing Li. *Security Challenges and Concerns of Internet of Things (IoT)*, pages 153–185. Springer International Publishing, Cham, 2019.
4. Rihab Chaari, Fatma Ellouze, Anis Koubaa, Basit Qureshi, Nuno Pereira, Habib Youssef, and Eduardo Tovar. Cyber-physical systems clouds: A survey. *Computer Networks*, 108:260–278, 2016.
5. Raj Chaganti, Deepti Gupta, and Naga Vemprala. Intelligent network layer for cyber-physical systems security. *arXiv preprint arXiv:2102.00647*, 2021.

6. Somali Chaterji, Parinaz Naghizadeh, Muhammad Ashraful Alam, Saurabh Bagchi, Mung Chiang, David Corman, Brian Henz, Suman Jana, Na Li, and Shaoshuai Mou. Resilient cyberphysical systems and their application drivers: A technology roadmap. NSF-supported workshop on Grand Challenges in Resilience, 2019.

7. Khurum Nazir Junejo and Jonathan Goh. Behaviour-based attack detection and classification in cyber physical systems using machine learning. In Proceedings of the 2nd ACM International Workshop on Cyber-Physical System Security, pages 34–43, 2016.

8. Zeeshan Ali Khan and Peter Herrmann. Recent advancements in intrusion detection systems for the internet of things. *Security and Communication Networks*, 19:1–19, 2019.

9. Jay Lee and Behrad Bagheri. Hung-an kao. A Cyber-physical systems architecture for Industry 4.0-based manufacturing systems, 4:18–23, 2015.

10. Bo Li and Lichen Zhang. Security analysis of cyber-physical system. In AIP Conference Proceedings, volume 1839, page 020-178. AIP Publishing LLC, 2017.

11. Sean Marston, Zhi Li, Subhajyoti Bandyopadhyay, Juheng Zhang, and Anand Ghalsasi. Cloud computing—the business perspective. *Decision Support Systems*, 51(1):176–189, 2011.

12. Dimitris Mourtzis. Simulation in the design and operation of manufacturing systems: state of the art and new trends. *International Journal of Production Research*, 58(7):1927–1949, 2020.

13. J Snehi, A Bhandari, V Baggan, and M Snehi. Diverse methods for signature based intrusion detection schemes adopted. *International Journal of Recent Technology and Engineering (IJRTE)*, 9(2):44–49, 2020.

14. Manish Snehi and Abhinav Bhandari. Apprehending mirai botnet philosophy and smart learning models for iot-ddos detection. In 2021 8th International Conference on Computing for Sustainable Global Development (INDIACom), pages 501–505. IEEE, 2021.

15. Manish Snehi and Abhinav Bhandari. Vulnerability retrospection of security solutions for software-defined cyber–physical system against ddos and iot-ddos attacks. *Computer Science Review*, 40:100371, 2021.

16. Mikel Uriarte, Jasone Astorga, Eduardo Jacob, Maider Huarte, and Oscar Lopez. *Survey on Access Control Models Feasible in Cyber-Physical Systems*, pages 103–152. Springer International Publishing, Cham, 2019.

17. J Verma, A Bhandari, and G Singh. Review of existing data sets for network intrusion detection system. *Advances in Mathematics: Scientific Journal*, 9(6):3849–3854, 2020.

18. Jyoti Verma, Abhinav Bhandari, and Gurpreet Singh. A metaanalysis of role of network intrusion detection systems in confronting network attacks. In 2021 8th International Conference on Computing for Sustainable Global Development (INDIACom), pages 506–511. IEEE, 2021.

19. Zhenhua Wang, Wei Xie, Baosheng Wang, Jing Tao, and Enze Wang. A survey on recent advanced research of CPS security. *Applied Sciences*, 11(9):3751, 2021.

20. Marcelo Yannuzzi, Rodolfo Milito, Rene Serral-GraciŒa, Diego Montero, and Mario Nemirovsky. Key ingredients in an iot recipe: Fog computing, cloud computing, and more fog computing. In 2014 IEEE 19th International Workshop on Computer Aided Modeling and Design of Communication Links and Networks (CAMAD), pages 325–329. IEEE, 2014.

5

Recent Advancements in the State of Cloud Security in Cyber Physical Systems

Jyoti Verma, Abhinav Bhandari and Gurpreet Singh

CONTENTS

Recent advancements in information technology and the ever-increasing sophistication of digital networks have compelled creation of the orchestration of intelligent technologies – cyber physical systems (CPSs). Cloud-based analysis in the CPS is a flexible and dependable architecture for performing analytics operations on large data streams, such as processing, aggregating, and analyzing data at various granularities. In a cyber physical cloud computing system, integrating cloud computing with heterogeneous networks creates a number of threats. This chapter discusses upcoming findings on cyber physical structures in the cloud world and recent advances in implementing machine learning and deep learning. We have studied cloud attack prevention models, a cloud-based CPS security framework, and the issues in the implementation of CPS at the cloud layer. Network intrusion detection systems (NIDSs) can be implemented at any IoT network's edge router, on a single or many hosts, or on each physical device to guarantee that possible attacks are detected.

DOI: 10.1201/9781003185543-5

5.1 Introduction

Cyber physical systems (CPSs) are now everywhere: in many consumer products such as robots, vehicles, and personal devices; energy systems such as smart grids; many civil infrastructures such as smart buildings and smart homes; industrial control systems such as nuclear plants, to name a few. They have also been seen as the future of information technology, reconstructing how people communicate with the physical systems. The internet transformed how people interact [39]. In recent years, CPS has gained popularity to enhance system performance instead of integrating software systems with embedded computer systems or sensor networks. CPS systems are designed to combine computing components, underlying networks, and physical components in a well-defined environment to achieve a specified goal and firmly combine computing elements and physical processes [21]. When working with physical systems, CPSs are distinguished by their stability, performance, consistency, robustness, flexibility, and efficiency. Cyber physical systems are systems in which calculations are inextricably linked with the physical environment, implying that physical data are the primary component driving computation. With the introduction of cloud computing and the internet of things (IoT), these CPSs now have a plethora of new opportunities to increase their capabilities by utilizing cloud resources in several ways. Networked computer systems, real-time control systems, wireless sensor/actuator networks, social networks, and cloud computing services are the five technologies at the heart of the CPS cloud idea. Cloud computing allows for network-based access to computational and data storage services on a pay-per-use basis. The cloud allows for improved resource use and, as a result, lower service access costs for people. Cloud services include software platform and infrastructure as a service. With the use of virtualization technologies, cloud computing virtualizes and dynamically distributes computing and data resources to a range of users based on their demands. Because cloud computing is a shared resource that can be accessed from anywhere, it is subject to a variety of threats, including host and network-based attacks, and so requires quick attention. Because of its distributed nature, the cloud environment is exposed to a huge variety of threats. The cloud computing paradigm enables highly accessible, dependable, and less expensive access to applications and services through the network.

Figure 5.1 presents the CPS cloud consisting of highly interconnected software components and physical objects. The interconnected components operate on different spatial and temporal dimensions, show numerous behavioral modalities, and interact with users and the system components. They can communicate with data sources and access services using various methods that alter their use context. Smart grids, global realms, remote monitoring systems, intelligent medical systems, border defense systems,

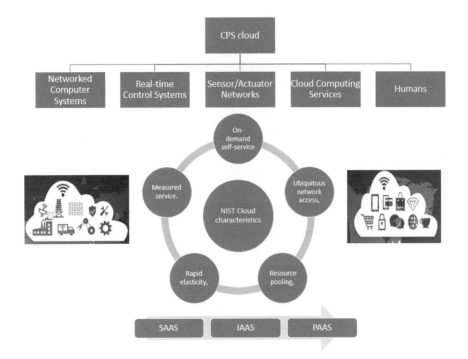

FIGURE 5.1
CPS cloud.

self-governing transport, and automated avionics are the critical applications of CPS. Recent deep learning methods have developed as influential computational standards. They have exhibited notable breakthroughs in dealing with an extensive volume of data in unsupervised contexts. Deep learning is transforming because it provides a practical learning design and enables the system to determine characteristics from data without explicitly devising them automatically. With the evolving CPS infrastructure technologies, particularly the IoT, wearables, cloud platform, and analytics on the stored data, there is potential for acquiring and processing a tremendous amount of data from the physical world. Advanced computing models and technologies (e.g., smart home or city) relating to context-aware systems, action identification, distributed intelligent sensing, analysis of big data, and deep learning have been increasingly evolved and fused into this CPS to present it as a reality [22].

The organization of the rest of the chapter is as follows. Section 5.2 presents the details of studied literature on significant security problems concerning the CPS cloud. Section 5.3 discusses the existing cyber physical cloud computing system security models, while Section 5.4 addresses the discussion and open challenges in the implementation of CPS at the cloud layer. Section 5.5 brings the survey to a close.

5.2 Literature Review of Major Security Issues Related to CPS Cloud

CPS must perform several tasks at various stages, including device protection, data communications, application development, and data storage. In CPS communication networks, data transmission security is critical for detecting imposters and harmful behavior. Basic security precautions are required [3]. Information security is concerned with securing data during data aggregation, processing, and large-scale sharing in a network context. The use of encryption, for example, emphasizes data protection in information security. Attacks against CPS have the potential to cause substantial physical harm to the environment. The CPS is subject to both passive and aggressive threats. Perception layer attacks include cyberattacks on nodes such as sensors and actuators [32]. Equipment or line failure, electromagnetic interference, differential power analysis, and information disclosure are examples of perception-layer attacks [35] (Figure 5.2). Significant threats

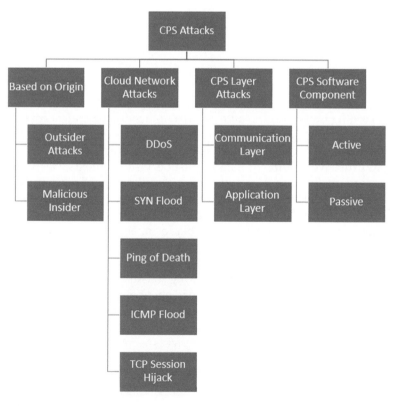

FIGURE 5.2
Cloud CPS attacks.

at the application layer include passive attacks such as user privacy leakage and control command forgery [33]. Passive security attacks are defined as those that offer some sort of access to the CPS but do not directly damage it. Active attacks change or harm the CPS in some way through replay attacks, modification, denial of service (DoS), masquerade, observation, and action assaults [5]. Several researchers have examined cloud computing security problems at various levels. Table 5.1 also includes a list of security solutions. Table 5.2 discusses CPS threats at various layers, their security requirements, and mechanisms.

Machine learning (ML) is a subset of contemporary artificial intelligence (AI). It is strongly related to (and frequently involves) computational statistics, focused on the prediction processes of computers. It is intimately connected with scientific and analytical optimization, developing methodologies, theory, and application fields. Machine learning is sometimes mistaken for data mining. Data mining is concerned with the exploratory exploration of data using unsupervised learning. Unsupervised algorithms are also included in machine learning, and they may be used to learn and construct baseline behavioral profiles for a variety of entities. It may then be used to identify severe irregularities [36]. Arthur Samuel, called the father of machine learning, defined it as a field of study that enables computers to learn without explicit instruction [16]. Machine learning is concerned with data categorization and regression models built based on accessible features learned from training data. Deep learning (DL) is a relatively new area of machine learning research. Its goal is to create a neural network that replicates the human

TABLE 5.1

Literature on cloud security concerns, threats, attacks, and security solutions for CPS Cloud

References	CPS cloud security issues and challenges	CPS cloud-based attacks	CPS cloud security risks	CPS cloud security issues and solutions	Solutions for threats in the CPS cloud
[40]	✓			✓	
[25]	✓	✓	✓	✓	✓
[8]					
[9]	✓	✓	✓	✓	✓
[34]					
[11]	✓	✓	✓	✓	
[15]	✓	✓		✓	
[41]	✓			✓	
[18]	✓				
[1]					
[24]	✓			✓	
[13]	✓	✓	✓	✓	✓
[30]	✓	✓	✓	✓	✓

TABLE 5.2

CPS threats at various layers, their security requirements, and mechanisms

Layers	Threats/Attacks	Security requirements	Security mechanisms
Application layer [29]	DoS/DDoS, cross-site scripting (XSS), injection attacks, buffer overflow, session hijacking, misconfiguring security protocols, missing to limit URL access	Authentication and key agreement, privacy protection, security education and management	Access control management, security management, privacy protection management
Support layer [16]	Data breaches/data loss, account hijacking, insecure APIs, denial of service, malicious insiders, abuse of cloud services, shared technology issues	Secure multi-party computation, secure cloud computing, anti-virus	Behavior entities certification, data metric key generation and distribution security and computation
Network layer [28]	Eavesdropping, data modification, identity spoofing, password-based attacks, man-in-the-middle attack, key compromise attack, data sniffing	Identity authentication, anti- DDoS, encryption mechanism, communication security	User privacy, data encryption, data integrity, multicast security, entity authentication, access security
Perceptual layer [7]	DDoS due to jamming, physical devices destruction, manipulation of physical assets	Light-weight encryption technology, protecting sensor data, key agreement	Intrusion detection, key management, secure routing, distributed authentication

brain and can do analytical learning. It promotes regular human brain activity associated with data comprehension, such as picture, sound, and natural language data learning. Hinton proposed the concept of DL, which is based on the Deep Belief Network (DBN) model. He presented an unsupervised aggressive training approach in the hope of resolving deep structure optimization concerns. Additionally, he presented a multilayer autoencoder's deep structure.

The convolutional neural network introduced by LeCun et al. [6] is the first true multilayer structure learning technique that takes advantage of a space-relative connection. The space-relative connection minimizes the number of parameters and hence increases training performance. Several machine learning algorithms are often employed, including KNN [17], SVM [19], Decision Tree [27], and Bayes [21]. The DL model is composed of the DBM [12], the CNN [26], and the LSTM. There are several settings to select from, including the number of layers and nodes, and enhance the model and integration. Following training, several alternative models must be examined on a variety of dimensions [23]. DL is a machine-learning technique that is built on the concept of data learning. An observation, such as a picture, can be described in various ways, either as a vector containing the intensity values of individual pixels or, more abstractly, as a sequence of edges, an area of a certain form, or the like. By utilizing unique representations, task learning via examples is facilitated. As with machine learning, deep learning approaches include both supervised and unsupervised learning. The learning models developed under various learning frameworks are fairly distinct. The advantage of deep learning is the ability to efficiently substitute features manually via unsupervised or semi-supervised feature learning and hierarchical feature extraction [38].

5.3 Study of Existing Cyber Physical Cloud Computing Systems Security Models

When cloud computing is combined with heterogeneous networks in a cyber physical computing system, a range of risks are introduced. Cyber physical attacks encompass physical space attacks, cyberspace attacks, and the interception, substitution, or erasure of data from communication systems [37]. Numerous intrusion detection and security strategies have been published and implemented for cloud security in the past source arshad2013novel[4]. The Table 5.3 summarizes security solutions offered by researchers over the past few decades for cloud security.

Numerous previously known methods for enhancing network security in dispersed or isolated systems have been explored, suggested, and implemented. Among the measures are firewalls, network intrusion detection, and prevention systems. It comprises cloud computing infrastructure, communication connectivity, and a wireless sensor network in a top-down architecture. Horizontal security decomposes the cyber physical cloud computing system (CPCCS) horizontally and protects each level. The horizontal security paradigm is based on a split of CPCCS components horizontally. The vertical security concept is based on the CPCCS layer hierarchy. It comprises cloud computing infrastructure, application layer XaaS communication links, and wireless sensor networks in a top-down hierarchy [2]. Vertical decomposition ensures that data collection occurs vertically. A profile-based network intrusion detection and prevention system for securing cloud environments focuses on a unique method of protecting cloud networks from hostile insiders and outsiders [14]. Network profiling creates a profile for each virtual machine (VM) in the cloud that identifies the network activities of each cloud user (assigned VM) [10]. The data obtained are then used to identify (identify) cloud network risks. The approach is unique in that it identifies network

TABLE 5.3

Security solutions proposed for CPS cloud security

Applications	Issues	Security solutions
Encryption and digital signatures with secure data placement on the cloud [27]	It involves data encryption/decryption before cloud storage, has a lengthy data retrieval time and is complicated in terms of data management and access	Secure data placement on cloud
Encryption and digital signatures cryptographic solutions	It has a high computational cost, a high-power consumption, an increase in latency, and restricted computational capabilities. It is effective only against fixed malicious actions	Cryptographic solutions
Data access permission restrictions with advanced security controls [15]	It must be used in conjunction with other solutions; it is insufficient to protect users' data on its own and may result in increased latency while accessing the data	Advanced security controls
Visualizing detection of anomalies with anomaly detection [20]	It requires a large training set, is expensive in terms of overhead and training data storage, and may require human analysts' assistance	Anomaly detection
Visualizing detection of anomalies with visualization techniques	It necessitates extensive statistical analysis of traffic and may require human supervision	Visualization techniques

assaults quickly and easily. The proposed technique may be used with minor modifications to existing cloud infrastructure, citing famous cloud computing security models such as those in [31]. It includes:

1. The cube model
2. Model for multi-tenancy
3. Model for risk evaluation

Numerous noncryptographic techniques have been proposed to mitigate and eliminate the possibilities of a cyberattack or other destructive occurrences. This was accomplished through the implementation of network intrusion detection systems (NIDS). Research activities were conducted to detect attacks on CPS. These attacks were classified into:

1. Anomaly Detection Model that describes standard CPS processes
2. Cyber-based methodology that is used to identify prospective threats.

Network intrusion detection systems can be deployed at the edge router of any particular IoT network, on a single or multiple hosts, or on each of the physical devices to ensure that potential attacks are detected.

5.4 Discussion and Open Issues in Implementation of CPS at Cloud Layer

There are several papers in the literature that explore cloud computing security problems. The aforementioned researches are confined to discussing security concerns and do not offer security solutions. Furthermore, the future topic has not been thoroughly explored, and an overview of cloud technology is lacking. One of the significant computational problems in maintaining data confidentiality and privacy protection is the semi- or fully autonomous security management for CPS at the cloud layer. Another concern is the high processing expenses of using encryption. The preservation of privacy is a crucial feature of big data analytics and mining. Research is required to evaluate their usefulness for different forms of large data, as well as their performance assessment and durability in various mining approaches. CPS must continually adapt to new conditions while running and functioning effectively with little or no human oversight due to the dynamic nature of the physical environment. CPS applications may need to work together to complete a certain objective. Work in these areas will considerably assist users in doing quantitative and technical analyses and making better decisions before migrating to the cloud. New low-complexity cryptographic techniques are required to secure CPS in real-time operations. There is a need for a new family of resource-constrained light-weight block or stream encryption algorithms to secure real-time CPS communications. There is a requirement for computing resources, verifiable backups, and CPS to be self-healing in order to recover rapidly from availability attacks. Network intrusion detection systems should be multifunctional in every way and should act in collaboration with firewalls.

5.5 Conclusion

Despite the numerous benefits of cloud computing, it raises security concerns, impeding cloud computing's rapid adoption. This chapter discussed forthcoming results on cyber physical architecture in the cloud realm, as well as current developments in machine learning and deep learning implementation. We investigated cloud attack prevention methods, as well as a CPS security architecture that is cloud-based. We discussed the security of cloud-based cyber physical networks, and the obstacles in implementing CPS at the cloud layer. We examined numerous components, risks and cyberattacks, as well as security requirements and processes relevant at various tiers of CPS cloud and proposed the deployment of network intrusion detection systems at the edge router of any particular IoT network to ensure the detection of potential attacks.

Bibliography

1. Mazhar Ali, Samee U Khan, and Athanasios V Vasilakos. Security in cloud computing: Opportunities and challenges. *Information Sciences*, 305:357–383, 2015.

2. Anees Ara, Mznah Al-Rodhaan, Yuan Tian, and Abdullah Al Dhelaan. A secure service provisioning framework for cyber physical cloud computing systems. *arXiv preprint arXiv:1611.00374*, 2015.

3. Faisal Arafsha, Fedwa Laamarti, and Abdulmotaleb El Saddik. Cyber-physical system framework for measurement and analysis of physical activities. *Electronics*, 8(2), 2019.

4. Junaid Arshad, Paul Townend, and Jie Xu. A novel intrusion severity analysis approach for clouds. *Future Generation Computer Systems*, 29(1):416–428, 2013.

5. Nari S Arunraj, Robert Hable, Michael Fernandes, Karl Leidl, and Michael Heigl. Comparison of supervised, semi-supervised and unsupervised learning methods in network intrusion detection system (nids) application. *Anwendungen und Konzepte der Wirtschaftsinformatik*, 6:10–19, 2017.

6. Yoshua Bengio, Yann LeCun, et al. Scaling learning algorithms towards AI. *Large-Scale Kernel Machines*, 34(5):1–41, 2007.

7. Waleed Bulajoul, Anne James, and Mandeep Pannu. Network intrusion detection systems in high-speed traffic in computer networks. In *2013 IEEE 10th International Conference on e-Business Engineering*, pages 168–175. IEEE, 2013.

8. Dylan Chou and Meng Jiang. Data-driven network intrusion detection: A taxonomy of challenges and methods. *arXiv preprint arXiv:2009.07352*, 2020.

9. Luigi Coppolino, Salvatore D'Antonio, Giovanni Mazzeo, and Luigi Romano. Cloud security: Emerging threats and current solutions. *Computers & Electrical Engineering*, 59:126–140, 2017.

10. Mostapha Derfouf and Mohsine Eleuldj. Performance analysis of intrusion detection systems in the cloud computing. In *2017 3rd International Conference of Cloud Computing Technologies and Applications (CloudTech)*, pages 1–8. IEEE, 2017.

11. Abhishek Divekar, Meet Parekh, Vaibhav Savla, Rudra Mishra, and Mahesh Shirole. Benchmarking datasets for anomaly-based network intrusion detection: Kdd cup 99 alternatives. In *2018 IEEE 3rd International Conference on Computing, Communication and Security (ICCCS)*, pages 1–8. IEEE, 2018.

12. Mohamed Amine Ferrag, Leandros Maglaras, Sotiris Moschoyiannis, and Helge Janicke. Deep learning for cyber security intrusion detection: Approaches, datasets, and comparative study. *Journal of Information Security and Applications*, 50:102–419, 2020.

13. Komal Singh Gill, Sharad Saxena, and Anju Sharma. Taxonomy of security attacks on cloud environment: A case study on telemedicine. In *2019 Amity International Conference on Artificial Intelligence (AICAI)*, pages 454–460. IEEE, 2019.

14. Sanchika Gupta, Padam Kumar, and Ajith Abraham. A profile based network intrusion detection and prevention system for securing cloud environment. *International Journal of Distributed Sensor Networks*, 9(3):364–575, 2013.

15. Salman Iqbal, Miss Laiha Mat Kiah, Babak Dhaghighi, Muzammil Hussain, Suleman Khan, Muhammad Khurram Khan, and Kim-Kwang Raymond Choo. On cloud security attacks: A taxonomy and intrusion detection and prevention as a service. *Journal of Network and Computer Applications*, 74:98–120, 2016.

16. Khurum Nazir Junejo and Jonathan Goh. Behaviour-based attack detection and classification in cyber physical systems using machine learning. In Proceedings of the 2nd ACM International Workshop on Cyber-Physical System Security, pages 34–43, 2016.

17. Farrukh Aslam Khan and Abdu Gumaei. A comparative study of machine learning classifiers for network intrusion detection. In *International Conference on Artificial Intelligence and Security*, pages 75–86. Springer, 2019.

18. A Khraisat, I Gondal, P Vamplew, et al. Survey of intrusion detection systems: Techniques, datasets and challenges. cybersecurity, 2(2019):20, 2019.

19. Kwangjo Kim and Muhamad Erza Aminanto. Deep learning in intrusion detection perspective: Overview and further challenges. In 2017 International Workshop on Big Data and Information Security (IWBIS), pages 5–10. IEEE, 2017.

20. Aditya Kuppa, Slawomir Grzonkowski, Muhammad Rizwan Asghar, and Nhien-An Le-Khac. Black box attacks on deep anomaly detectors. In *Proceedings of the 14th International Conference on Availability, Reliability and Security*, pages 1–10, 2019.

21. Nour Moustafa, Benjamin Turnbull, and Kim-Kwang Raymond Choo. An ensemble intrusion detection technique based on proposed statistical flow features for protecting network traffic of internet of things. *IEEE Internet of Things Journal*, 6(3):4815–4830, 2018.

22. Prem Prakash, Jayaraman Lizhe, and Albert Y Zomaya Editors. *Handbook of Integration of Cloud Computing, Cyber Physical Systems and Internet of Things*. Springer, 2020.

23. Rojalina Priyadarshini and Rabindra Kumar Barik. A deep learning based intelligent framework to mitigate DDoS attack in fog environment. *Journal of King Saud University-Computer and Information Sciences*, 34(3):825–831, 2019.

24. Deepak Puthal, Bibhudutta PS Sahoo, Sambit Mishra, and Satyabrata Swain. Cloud computing features, issues, and challenges: A big picture. In 2015 International Conference on Computational Intelligence and Networks, pages 116–123. IEEE, 2015.

25. Tarek Radwan, Marianne A Azer, and Nashwa Abdelbaki. Cloud computing security: Challenges and future trends. *International Journal of Computer Applications in Technology*, 55(2):158–172, 2017.

26. RK Rahul, T Anjali, Vijay Krishna Menon, and KP Soman. Deep learning for network flow analysis and malware classification. In International Symposium on Security in Computing and Communication, pages 226–235. Springer, 2017.

27. Kajal Rai, M Syamala Devi, and Ajay Guleria. Decision tree based algorithm for intrusion detection. *International Journal of Advanced Networking and Applications*, 7(4):2828, 2016.

28. M Mazhar Rathore, Awais Ahmad, and Anand Paul. Real time intrusion detection system for ultra-high-speed big data environments. *The Journal of Supercomputing*, 72(9):3489–3510, 2016.

29. Swathi Sambangi and Lakshmeeswari Gondi. A machine learning approach for ddos (distributed denial of service) attack detection using multiple linear regression. *Multidisciplinary Digital Publishing Institute Proceedings*, 51:2–12, 2020.

30. Dinesh Singh, Dhiren Patel, Bhavesh Borisaniya, and Chirag Modi. Collaborative ids framework for cloud. *International Journal of Network Security*, 18(4):699–709, 2016.

31. J Snehi, A Bhandari, V Baggan, and M Snehi. Diverse methods for signature based intrusion detection schemes adopted. *International Journal of Recent Technology and Engineering (IJRTE)*, 9(2):44–49, 2020.

32. Manish Snehi and Abhinav Bhandari. Apprehending mirai botnet philosophy and smart learning models for iot-ddos detection. In *2021 8th International Conference on Computing for Sustainable Global Development (INDIACom)*, pages 501–505. IEEE, 2021.

33. Manish Snehi and Abhinav Bhandari. Vulnerability retrospection of security solutions for software-defined cyber–physical system against ddos and iot-ddos attacks. *Computer Science Review*, 40:100-371, 2021.

34. Yunchuan Sun, Junsheng Zhang, Yongping Xiong, and Guangyu Zhu. Data security and privacy in cloud computing. *International Journal of Distributed Sensor Networks*, 10(7):190-903, 2014.

35. Thomas H-J Uhlemann, Christian Lehmann, and Rolf Steinhilper. The digital twin: Realizing the cyber-physical production system for industry 4.0. *Procedia Cirp*, 61:335–340, 2017.

36. J Verma, A Bhandari, and G Singh. Review of existing data sets for network intrusion detection system. *Advances in Mathematics: Scientific Journal*, 9(6):3849–3854, 2020.

37. Jyoti Verma, Abhinav Bhandari, and Gurpreet Singh. A meta-analysis of role of network intrusion detection systems in confronting network attacks. In *2021 8th International Conference on Computing for Sustainable Global Development (INDIACom)*, pages 506–511. IEEE, 2021.

38. Yang Xin, Lingshuang Kong, Zhi Liu, Yuling Chen, Yanmiao Li, Hongliang Zhu, Mingcheng Gao, Haixia Hou, and Chunhua Wang. Machine learning and deep learning methods for cybersecurity. *IEEE Access*, 6:35365–35381, 2018.

39. Qiuxia Yang and Lichen Zhang. A framework for complex cloud-integrated CPSs. 147(Ncce):963–965, 2018.

40. Minqi Zhou, Rong Zhang, Wei Xie, Weining Qian, and Aoying Zhou. Security and privacy in cloud computing: A survey. In *2010 Sixth International Conference on Semantics, Knowledge and Grids*, pages 105–112. IEEE, 2010.

41. Dimitrios Zissis and Dimitrios Lekkas. Addressing cloud computing security issues. *Future Generation Computer Systems*, 28(3):583–592, 2012.

6

A Comprehensive Review: Detection and Mitigation Solutions of DDoS Attacks in CPS

Jagdeep Singh and Navjot Jyoti

CONTENTS

As technology is growing at a faster pace, societal dependence on online services/applications is also increasing. Technology is changing almost every domain. The new way to integrate the physical processes with computation using networking is coined as cyber physical systems (CPSs), where advanced embedded computers control and monitor the physical processes. However, research has reached the advanced level to secure the systems, yet, wherever networking is involved in any system, vulnerabilities lead the system to become the victim of cyberattacks. The most disturbing cyberattack is Distributed Denial of Service (DDoS) attacks that compromise online resources' availability. There are many vulnerabilities in CPSs that make these systems a major victim of DDoS and DoS attacks. Hence, the study of DDoS attacks and their defense solutions are active areas of research. In this chapter, the authors reviewed the detection and mitigation solutions for DDoS attacks in CPSs, which would help fellow researchers to understand

DOI: 10.1201/9781003185543-6

the state of the art of existing vulnerabilities and solutions for the same. Authors also tried to find the research gaps in existing methods so that solutions could be designed as more efficient and robust in future.

6.1 Introduction

Today's technology is continually growing at a faster pace and evolving connectivity between various devices; consequently it allows the devices to collect various types of information to optimize the working of the system. This interconnectivity of the devices often refers to the IoT (internet of things). IoT devices are those that are connected to the internet, such as devices with applications in transportation, health care, energy, manufacturing, power generation, and many more [1].

In many applications, IoT technology helps to improve the performance of the systems. For example, IoT medical devices collect patients' data and help the medical professional to take better care of patients. This integration of real-world physical components with cyber components using sensors, computing, and network technologies known as CPS [2, 3] yields many benefits for society. Since 2006, the NFS (National Science Foundation) has provided grants for research on CPSs. Numerous colleges and foundations (e.g., UCB, Memphis, Vanderbilt, Notre Dame, Michigan, General Motors Research, Maryland, and Development Center) have joined these research projects [4, 5]. The CPS is the complex multidimensional arrangement of a coordinated processing, network, and actual physical environment. It improves the limit of the framework from numerous angles, for example, data handling, real-time communication, controlling from remote sites, part-free coordination unit, and actual physical objects in a profoundly incorporated and intuitive network environment through a set of calculations [6, 7].

CPSs are intricate, huge, and organized blend of sensors, actuators, and computing nodes that monitor and control physical processes [8]. They work on physical and digital levels at the same time for improved execution. The main parts of CPSs involve sensors and actuators. The information from sensors is gathered and provided to the digital part or the network layer, which sends the suitable reaction to the actuators of the system. Accordingly, the physical qualities of the framework are controlled through the network-dependent readings gathered from the sensors.

With the arrival of IoT devices, Industry 4.0 brought an assembly of IoT devices, enterprise environment, and control framework infrastructure in the business together. IoT has empowered regular items to be brainy and communicable [9]. The researchers and manufacturers are carrying out the development of the CPS similarly. The CPS and Industry v4.0 together offer significant monetary potential [10]. For instance, the German gross worth will be boosted by a cumulative 267 billion Euros by 2025 upon introducing the CPS into Industry v4.0 [11].

Due to the high complexity and heterogeneous behavior of CPSs, because of cyber and physical aspects, a CPS has many general and application-specific vulnerabilities that can be exploited by an assailant to perform devilish activities [12]. Since CPSs control the physical process remotely, the results of a cyberattack may be irreversible and disastrous depending upon the seriousness of the assault and application domain. Thus, disrupting CPSs brings about a considerable loss of the economy, and, consequently, its security should be of fundamental significance.

The development and omnipresence of technologies have turned up many issues and difficulties to society. Numerous cyberattacks can be launched against the network, which compromise the integrity, privacy, and availability of the network resources. The most perilous security attacks are Denial of Service (DoS) attacks and their variations which compromise the system availability and raze the network resources. Furthermore, Distributed Denial of Service (DDoS) assaults occur when numerous devices strike in a coordinated manner. The main aim of these attacks is to exhaust the network or server resources until the system fails to deliver its natural services to the legitimate user in a timely fashion. DoS attacks are easy to defend once the attack source is determined by blocking the traffic from the source end. However, DDoS attacks are more potent as there are multiple distributed compromised machines involved which are more difficult to determine than a single machine. The effect of DDoS attacks manifolds by overwhelming and geographically distributed IoT devices as IoT devices are most vulnerable [13].

In literature, many methodologies have been proposed by researchers to combat the problem of the above-said cyberattacks. A comprehensive survey of all existing techniques for detecting and mitigating DDoS attacks and findings of the research gaps in existing solutions could provide better future directions in designing more robust methodologies. This chapter aims to provide a comprehensive literature survey and find some valid research gaps so that fellow researchers could use these directions in the betterment of designing defense solutions for CPSs.

6.2 Overview of CPS

This term was coined by Helen Gill in 2006 at the National Science Foundation (NSF) CPS workshop led by the US National Science Foundation [14]. When the idea was presented, it got the world's attention for its in-depth research from various researchers worldwide at different levels, from system design, CPS theory, and operation environment. As the CPS was complex architecture, the integration of technological developments brought much more attention than expected. Different researchers have varying levels of definition of Cyber Physical Systems, However as per the reference [15]:

> CPSs comprise interacting digital, analog, physical, and human components engineered for function through integrated physics and logic.

Lee [16] thinks that the CPS is a series of calculation processes, and it is the tight amalgamation of physical process modules by computing the core to monitor the task of the physical entity. Moreover, it is also the perception of the environment utilizing control and network and computing components. Behati et al. [6] believe that the CPS is an exceedingly reliable system between diverse computing and physical elements of the system, which are closely integrated and coordinated with each other dynamically. Krogh et al. accept, by looking at various computing and information storage processing levels, that CPSs are a combination of communications, computing, and storage capacity, which are further able to look after the networked computer systems of many entities in the real world. Branicky et al. consider that cyber is included in physical processes and combines communication and control technology [18]. Wenfand [19] accepts that it can compute physically equipped systems of scalable networked devices. The idea is based on depth fusion and environmental perceptions. The CPS is able to control the influence of the feedback loop using computation and physical process; therefore, it achieves real-time interaction and in-depth fusion. Zhongjie [7] pointed out that the CPS stresses cyber physical interaction. It contains a large amount of heterogeneous data and uncertain information about the network environment, which is reliable for signal processing and communications. Therefore, the next generation of intelligent structures would be able to realize the interconnection of the real physical world and virtual world. From the computer science perspective, CPSs are the reconciliation of computing and actual processes. They incorporate embedded PCs, network screens, and controllers, for the most part with input, where physical processes influence the calculations and the other way around [20]. In the same way, many other researchers pointed out the CPS from their field's point of view.

6.2.1 Architecture of CPS

There is no unified idea of the architecture of CPSs. For the most part, the CPS is characterized as combining the cyber world and the dynamic physical world. The CPS sees the actual physical world, processes the data using PCs, and influences and changes the physical world. He Jifeng [21] introduced the ideas of 3Cs: Computation, Communication, and Control (as shown in Figure 6.1). Considering data as a key component in CPS, it provides the

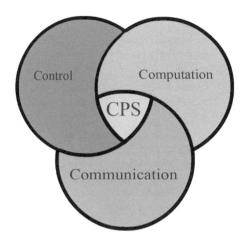

FIGURE 6.1
Components of a CPS.

constant detection, control and data admiminstration in the large scale systems. CPSs have close associations with embedded systems, sensors, and wireless network; however, they have their own attributes, for instance, the intricacy and dynamics of the environment, the enormous problem space and solution space are firmly related to the environment, and the prerequisite for high dependability of the framework. In the beginning phase, CPSs had a two-level structure: computing part and physical part. The physical part contains the sensors, which collect the data by sensing the physical world and execute decisions using the computing part. Further, the computing part analyzes and executes the data for decision-making, which was collected from the physical world. La et al. [22] coined the idea of the three-tier architecture of the CPS: environmental tier, service tier, and control tier (as shown in Figure 6.2). In this architecture, the environmental tier contains physical devices and sensors, which are used to access the physical environment for data gathering. The service tier is a typical computing component with some services in a services-oriented environment. Furthermore, the third tier of the CPS, i.e., the control tier, receives the data, which is monitored using devices in the physical tier. Furthermore, these data are used to make some controlling decisions, find the right services by consulting the service framework, and finally invoke the services in the physical tier as per decisions.

The typical functions of the system, such as decision-making, APIs to consumers, task scheduling, and task analysis, are performed in the service tier. The number of such services interacts and is deployed in the tier. The execution tier is another tier that interacts with the physical environment. This tier contains the actuators, which behave as per decisions made by execution and control tiers. The last part of this architecture, security assurance,

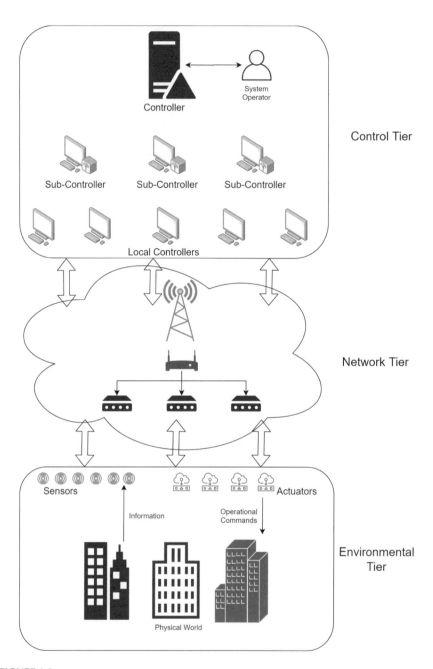

FIGURE 6.2
Typical three-tier architecture of the CPS.

is to ensure the security of different parts of the CPSs. Hu et al. proposed a new architecture having five components based on SOA (Service-Oriented Architecture). SOA is a variable-integrating model used to integrate loosely coupled services into one workflow. This generic CPS architecture has five tiers: perceive tier, data tier, service tier, execution tier, and security assurance component. Perceive tier contains the sensors to capture the data and provide the data to the data tier. The functionality of this tier is basically achieved using sensors and data pre-processing. Storage and computational devices are placed in the data tier. Its basic function is to provide heterogeneous data processing, such as noise reduction, normalization, data storage, and other similar functions. The typical functions of the system, such as decision-making, APIs to consumers, task scheduling, and task analysis, are performed in the service tier.

As mentioned at the beginning of this section, there is no uniform architecture of the CPS. The levels and layers of any CPS are mainly dependent and characterized by its area of application. The general idea of the CPS is to collaborate the cyber and physical worlds to improve the performance of the system. The three-tier architecture is the most acceptable form of the CPS [7].

6.2.2 Features of CSP

Although CPSs have a close relationship with embedded systems, they are different from embedded systems. They have their own characteristics that make them a slightly different framework. Some common characteristics [23–26] of the CPS are as follows:

1. *Closely Integrated*: CPSs are the mixtures of calculation and physical processes.
2. *Cyber Ability in Each Physical Segment*: The software is implanted in each installed framework or physical segment, and the framework assets like computing, network transfer speed, and so forth are generally restricted.
3. Networking at numerous scales: In CPSs, networking is at multiple scales, which incorporate wireless/wired networks, GSM, Bluetooth, WLAN, and so forth.
4. They are complex at various fleeting and spatial scales. The diverse part has likely in-equable granularity of time and spatiality, and they are stringently obliged by spatiality and real time.
5. Dynamically Redesigning/Re-configuring. CPSs are extremely complicated frameworks due to their diverse applications, so they should have versatile abilities.
6. The operation should be reliable and certified sometimes. As an extensive scope/complex framework, the reliability and security are fundamental requirements for CPSs.

6.3 Security Threats for CPS

Whenever a network is involved in any system, there must be some security concerns because the data travel through the network media and could be breached by intruders. Vulnerabilities in each layer of the network may cause some serious problems and loss to the system. These vulnerabilities always keep the space for cybercriminals for their malicious activities. In the three-tier architecture of the CPS, the network is the fundamental component. Therefore, each tier has vulnerabilities and has some severe threats to the CPS layers, as discussed below.

6.3.1 Security Threats for the Environmental Tier

The environmental layer is one of the significant sources of data and control statement execution sites. Most of the network devices are implemented in an unattended environment in the environment layer, and these devices can undoubtedly be the objective of an assailant. Capabilities of the devices, such as processing, communication, and storage capacity, are always limited; consequently, it is not easy to apply the traditional security mechanisms directly in this layer. Major threats for this layer are:

1. *Physical Attacks*: These attacks are the type of physical destruction of devices, resulting in loss of information, disclosure of sensitive data, etc.

2. *Component Failure*: Due to aging of the devices, external forces, or power line failures, devices cannot typically perform, which leads to degradation of the performance of the CPS.

3. *Electromagnetic Interference*: There are chances that due to unnecessary electromagnetic interference or disturbance from the environment, the useful electromagnetic signals may face severe problems to reach the receiver end, which leads to the deterioration of the working of the existing system/devices/transmission media.

4. *DoS (Denial of Service) Attacks*: These kinds of attacks may consume the whole bandwidth by occupying the capacity of the transmission channel using malicious traffic, which further stops the legitimate users' request to reach the server end.

6.3.2 Security Threats for the Network Tier

The network tier of the CPS plays an essential role. All the devices that collected the data in the environmental tier are traveling through the network tier. The architecture of this "next-generation network" carries some serious threats with its method of access and configuration of network devices. The vast amount of network traffic and a large number of nodes in this tier make this system vulnerable to many security threats, as discussed below.

1. *DoS/DDoS Attacks*: By intentionally sending malicious traffic, attackers can overwhelm the particular machine or system. Consequently, devices in the CPS would not be able to serve the normal traffic, and legitimate users would face denial of services. There are DoS attacks such as control network DoS attacks, flood attacks, and misleading direction attacks. In a control network attack, the attacker overwhelms the devices which are handing the control commands of the CPS. This attack makes the device unable to make the decision timely by keeping busy with malicious data. In flood attacks, the resources of the target system might be exhausted with the malevolent data, and resources would not be available for normal users. In misleading direction attacks, some of the compromised nodes change the destination and source address, leading to the movement of data in the wrong direction.

2. *Aggregation Node Attack*: There is a sink node in the system which is the core node of the existing system. By overwhelming or compromising the core node, the attack could harm the whole system.

3. *Black-Hole Attacks*: Sometimes the attacker adds a malicious node to the system with the false available channel information, which is then used to collect the route request packets, which could be used for harmful purposes.

6.3.3 Security Threats for the Application Tier

This tier of the CPS contains multiple applications that collect the users' data and keeps that data for authentication purposes. So there are many chances of stealing or misuse of the users' private data. The threats related to users' data privacy are also a concern for the researchers in the CPS. Some major threats to this tier are as below.

1. *Leakage of Users' Data*: Personal data of users, records, or other data might be collected through applications. Although there is secure data transmission, presentation, and storage, there are chances of leakage of the users' private data such as health status, spending habits, and bank details.

2. *Unauthorized Access*: Developers have tried their best to implement the security using passwords, captchas, and IDS (intrusion detection system). However, due to technological advancements, attackers have enough intelligent tools to breach the security and access the systems in many ways, leading to unauthorized access to the CPS's sensitive data.

3. *DoS/DDoS Attacks*: These attacks also harm the system in the application tier. By compromising the users' devices, attackers are inserting malicious codes into their machines without the awareness of the user. Then they may use the applications to generate the fake traffic toward the core nodes or a single transmission channel to overwhelm it.

4. *Forged Control Commands*: Attackers can also generate bogus commands to the service end, leading to the actuator behaving on the wrong signals.

6.4 DDoS Attacks and Its Reasons

A DDoS attack is an intentional attempt using multiple compromised geographically distributed machines to exhaust the resources of the online service provider by malicious traffic so that victims may not be able to provide their services to legitimate users. These machines are compromised using some malicious code such as Trojans, and the network of these machines is known as a botnet under the control of bot-master. In a DDoS attack, the ability of each compromised machine is combined and used against a particular device by the bot-master (who has control of every compromised machine). Figure 6.3 shows the basic working of the DDoS attack. Here we can observe that a bot-master, or the attacker, has access to some machines (which play the role of masters in attack), which are further connected to the other machines (which play the role of slaves in attack), and they make an active botnet under the control of single bot-master. After that, a bot-master is able to instruct multiple machines using a common command to generate fake traffic toward the victim. As a result, the traffic of genuine users would not be able to reach the victim machine, and the users will face denial of services.

Many reasons manifold the growth of the DDoS attacks, such as technological advancements, availability of user-friendly attack tools, and cheaper botnet-for-hire services [27]. The basic reasons for the rapid growth of DDoS attacks are as follows:

1. *Availability of Attack Tools*: Nowadays, DDoS attacks are easy to launch without any technical knowledge. There are many free tools, such as LOIC, XOIC, DDoSIM, and Pyloris, available to launch DDoS attacks with a single click without any technical knowledge, as well as botnets-for-hire services are cheaply available for the attackers, which leads to more potential for the nontechnical individuals to involve in such malicious activities.

2. *Variety of DDoS Attacks*: Attackers are equipped with more intelligent techniques and tools to elude the exiting IDSs. They can now

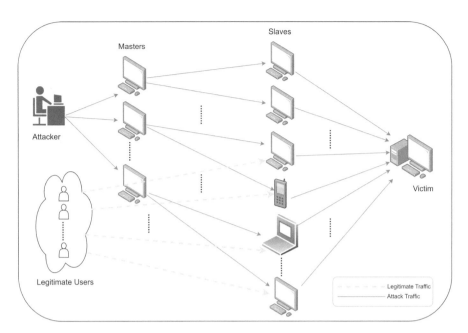

FIGURE 6.3
A typical DDoS scenario.

generate various types of attack packets so that existing defense methods may not be able to find common characteristics to differentiate the attack packets from normal packets. Attacks are able to mimic the behavior of the normal traffic with fake traffic and hence make it difficult to detect DDoS attacks.

3. *Spoofing of IPs*: The attackers are now spoofing their IP addresses with legitimate ones so that they can hide their identity while attacking. In this way, it is challenging to trace back the source of the DDoS attack, which encourages the attackers to commit such crimes without any fear. On the other hand, defense mechanisms are not able to block the spoofed IPs because these are legitimate ones, and ultimately it is again challenging to mitigate the impact of the DDoS attacks.

4. *High Volume of Traffic*: With the rapid growth of the use of online services, the number of online devices has also increased manifold. Consequently, bot-masters having large botnets as users of such online devices are not much aware of these technical issues, and their devices could be easily compromised. This leads to the creation of a high volume of fake traffic, and it is not easy to process every packet of the traffic at such speed as it is coming, and hence defense solutions start dropping legitimate packets too.

A wide range of systems is involved in the CPS, where the integration of the communication components is performed with the physical components. There are chances that these systems would face some problems or attacks as control components of CPSs are connected through the network environment. Here, traditional defense solutions could not cope with these issues; hence many research scholars are devoting their efforts to find the solutions to handle the cyber issues in CPSs [28–34]. Among the various attack types, such as DDoS attack, replay attack, deception attack, and triumphant attack, DDoS attacks are more potent attacks and can give rise to severe consequences [35, 36].

6.5 DDoS Attack Defence Solutions

In 2003, Cowan et al. [37] and Shacham et al. [38] gave the idea to protect code injection in real-time systems. Their method was designed for 64-bit space and could be easily defeated using 8/16/32 bit space. With advancements in the techniques and tools, control networks have also become a major target of malicious attacks. Yang et al. [39] (2005) introduced two basic techniques for intrusion detection based on anomaly detection and signature detection approaches for monitoring critical process systems, such as nuclear power plants. They used the auto-associative kernel regression (AAKR) model coupled with the statistical probability ratio test (SPRT) and applied this model in the simulation environment for its validity. The authors showed that their techniques could detect common types of cyberattacks such as ping flood, jolt2 attacks, bubonic attacks, simultaneous jolt2, and bubonic attacks. In this technique, the authors used the AAKR model to capture the system's normal behavior. After that, current observations are compared with the model's predicted observations, and a sequential probability ratio test is applied to determine whether it is normal behavior or anomalous behavior. In 2007, Cheung et al. [40] devised other model-based techniques to characterize the expected/acceptable behavior of the system from the anomalous behavior caused by attacks. The authors assumed that the process control systems have some properties such as protocols, static topologies, a limited number of applications and traffic patterns and believed that model-based monitoring has more power to detect unknown attacks for monitoring Modbus TCP. First, based on the Modbus application protocol and TCP implementation guide specifications, the authors employed protocol-level models to detect the exploiting of an unknown backdoor or a denial-of-service attempt. Second, the expected communication patterns model is used to respond to the TCP connection of the Modbus server only. If the server would be compromised, then its attempt would violate the model, and thus, it can be detected. The third approach is used by authors is detecting changes in server or service availability. This method can detect the attempts of the server if they are not able to serve successfully. They validate their approach at the SCADA testbed at SNL, in which they used Bayes sensor, eXpert-Net, and Snort and sensors specific to Modbus TCP or to the monitoring environment. Amin et al. (2009) [41] developed a semi-definite programming base defense solution for denial-of-service attack against the discrete-time linear dynamical control systems. First, authors introduced safety constraints as basic security requirements for the system. Second, they used traditional uncertainty classes for generalization to incorporate more realistic attacks in the adversary model. This model aims to maximize the satisfaction of safety specifications with maximum probability along with power limitations. Authors used dynamic and convex programming as tools for their analysis. In addition, they modeled two types of attacks in their development: deception attacks and DoS attacks. When the components receive false data and believe it to be accurate, the situation is under the deception attack. In this attack, the attacker can compromise some sensors or controllers and supply false information such as an incorrect measurement, the false sender identity, or the incorrect timestamp from these devices.

On the other hand, attackers could also stop the accessibility of some of the components of the system. Lack of availability of any component means the situation is under the DoS attack. The attacker can jam the communication channels, attack the routing protocols, compromise devices and prevent them from sending data, flood with network traffic some devices, etc., to launch the DoS attacks. In 2010, Zimmer et al. [42] improved the idea of the aforementioned methods and used them to detect the intrusion in the cyber physical system using time stamps. The authors developed three mechanisms as T-Rex (Timed Return Execution), T-ProT (Timed Progress Tracking), and T-Axt (Timed Address Execution Tracking), which utilized the analysis of real-time applications for the detection of execution of unofficial code. They have proved the effectiveness of the system in hardware and software platforms. The timing metrics are used to detect the security breaches by comparing the metrics with the worst-case bounds of the application where applications exceed their timing requirements before the actual timing deadline miss. The detection of the intrusion at a fine-grained level is performed using a T-Rex module. The T-Rex component detects the delays of 5–22 cycles delay caused by code injections. T-ProT is used as intra-task checkpoints for the detection of coarser-grain injections between 9 and 5,000 cycles. Moreover, finally, T-AxT exploits asynchronous scheduler-triggered timing validations of application code sections without requiring instrumentation. Premaratne et al. [43] (2010) proposed an IDS (Intrusion Detection System) to counter the problem of the cyber threats for an IEC61850-automated substation, particularly based on the simulated attacks on IED (Intelligent Electronic Devices). They developed the detection system using data simulating by attacks and packet sniffing with forged ARP (Address Resolution Protocol). The authors devised rules by analyzing the collected data, such as more FTP session than their expected limit could indicate a DoS attack, more than 100 or 1,000 packets per second would be an indication of suspicious behavior or APR sniffer, respectively, larger ICMP packets could be an indicator of ping DoS attack, and a high number of login attempts would be suspicious behavior to ftp password crack attack, etc. They converted these rules into rules of Snort syntax for detection of malicious behavior of the system. They developed a simulation environment for the validation of their technique. Gao et al. [44] (2010) developed an intrusion detection system based on a neural network to detect the artifacts of command and response injection attacks by analyzing the physical behavior of the control system. They used a data set from the MSU SCADA Security Laboratory water tank control system to validate their approach. In this approach, the authors used a back-propagation algorithm to build the neural network, which can classify the network transaction as normal or abnormal. They used four features such as water level expressed as a percentage, command response frequency, mode of the operation of the control system, and the state of the water tank of the control system as input of the neural network. They experimented with various scenarios and got the accuracy of their method above 96% in each scenario.

Yuan et al. (2013) [45] designed a method based on value iteration methods and linear matrix inequalities for the calculation of the security policy for cyber physical control systems under DoS attacks. They used power systems to illustrate their design principle of the IDS. The authors established a hybrid discrete-time dynamical system model at the cyber layer and the underlying physical layer dynamical system. They used a discrete-time model with sensor-to-controller (S-C), and controller-to-actuator (C-A) delays to capture the dynamics of the physical layer, and the Markov chain is used for capturing the state of the cyber layer. Moreover, the authors provide an algorithm based on value iterations and LMIs (Linear Ma-trix Inequalities) for the calculation of the H^∞ optimal control and the cyber-security policy. Zhu et al. [46] used an algorithm with slight modifications based on receding-horizon control methodology to develop the IDS for the resilience of DoS attacks for the operator-vehicle network. Initially, they proposed their techniques for the replay attacks, but they used this technique for the denial-of-service with slight modifications to the existing technique. When the attacker erases the control commands sent from the operator, the vehicle would not receive anything, and the vehicle could detect the presence of the DoS attack by verifying the receipt of control commands at each time instant. Su et al. [47] proposed a novel approach to detect the behavior of DoS attackers using packet reception rate. The authors analyze the relationship among some system features, such as attack times, attack success rate, packet reception rate, and time window for the attack detection information. Using this information further, the authors proposed a compensation mechanism that can restore the system's state. They have shown the effectiveness using numerical and practical examples. They used anomaly-based techniques to characterize the anomalous behavior of the system. Hussain et al. [16] developed a consolidated framework for early detection of distributed denial of service attacks by utilizing deep convolutional neural networks. They designed their scheme to counter the problem of silent call, signaling, SMS spamming, or a blend of these attacks in CPSs. They used an open data set released by Telecom Italia in 2015, consisting of over 319 million real CDRs (Call Detail Records). They preprocess the raw data of CDRs and create an image from the whole data set for experimentation. Further, they send this image to the CNN model where ID(s) in the test image forward to the CN for further necessary actions. They proved more than 91% normal and underattack accuracy of their framework with experimentation.

6.6 Security Challenges

CPSs are more sophisticated systems and have a very high potential for the creation of new markets as well as for providing better solutions to the social risks; however, they need high demands on safety, security, quality, and privacy. There are several developments in the field of DDoS attacks detection, and mitigation has been done. However, with the growth of IoT-based devices, the network traffic is increasing exponentially, leading to the difficulty in handling high-volume traffic by existing devices and defense solutions. This scenario has brought many security challenges that need immediate attention to defend existing and future networking devices and applications. The major challenges in the security of the CPSs are as follows

1. *The Vast Amount of Network Traffic:* With the rapid growth in IoT-based devices, the network has become very complex and unstable; therefore, traditionally DDoS attacks and defense methods cannot handle the security efficiently. Moreover, devices are heterogeneous and geographically distributed and produce a massive amount of network traffic in a concise period, which is difficult to handle without new technologies like big data analytics. Handling today's network efficiently along with consideration of the performance of a system is a major challenge in front of the researcher community.

2. *Lack of Real-Time Experiment Set-Ups:* In recent times, plenty of solutions have been developed and validated by fellow researchers. However, an exponential increase in the frequency of attacks along with size makes these validations ineffective. Many existing solutions have been validated in simulated environments, but it is challenging to simulate today's high-volume traffic network. Therefore, this is another challenge for the researchers to devise the real-time experimental set-up to validate defense solutions.

3. *Lack of Availability of Benchmarked Data Sets:* Many researchers have used old data sets for the validation of their DDoS attack defense solutions. However, these data sets do not reflect the existing network scenario because network traffic has increased manifolds. So, the availability of the standard data set for validation of futuristic defense solutions is another challenge.

4. *CPS Component Authentication:* There are multiple components working in coordination. Every component has a vital role in the system. However, there must be some authentication mechanisms to authenticate the participation of each component in the system. Along with this, there must be the implementation of secured channels between sensors and controllers. These two aspects can increase the security of CPSs from any tempering. The development of such components is also a critical challenge for the research community.

6.7 Conclusion

The CPS transforms the way of interaction between human beings and the physical environment by integrating the physical processes with control processes through networking. The enhancement of the availability and reliability of the products and services is the main aim of the CPSs. However, CPSs are prone to various security vulnerabilities, leading to degradation of the system's efficiency, reliability, and safety. In this chapter, first we gave an overview of the CPS, along with its architecture. Then we saw the various security threats at different layers of the CPS. Then we focused on DDoS attacks and their reasons. Finally, we reviewed various defense solutions developed by researchers to handle DDoS attacks in CPSs. Although the researchers' community is working hard to defend against cyberattacks, these attacks are difficult to detect and mitigate due to a large number of geographically distributed devices that cause a significant amount of network traffic. In the future, it is suggested to devise realistic experimental set-ups for validations of the defense solutions and defense solutions to cope with the existing vulnerabilities of the CPSs.

Bibliography

1. Daniele Miorandi, Sabrina Sicari, Francesco De Pellegrini, and Imrich Chlamtac. Internet of things: Vision, applications and research challenges. *Ad hoc Networks*, 10(7):1497–1516, 2012.

2. Sherali Zeadally and Nafaßa Jabeur. Cyber-physical system design with sensor networking technologies. *The Institution of Engineering and Technology*, 2016.
3. Seyed Hossein Hosseini Nazhad Ghazani, Jalil Jabari Lotf, and RM Aliguliyev. A study on qos models for mobile adhoc networks. *International Journal of Modeling and Optimization*, 2(5):634, 2012.
4. J Sprinkle, U Arizona, and SS Sastry. Chess: Building a cyber-physical agenda on solid foundations. *Presentation Report*, 2008.
5. William G. Gilroy. https://news.nd.edu/news/nsf-funds-cyber-physical-systems-project/, Oct 2010.
6. Radhakisan Baheti and Helen Gill. Cyber-physical systems. *The Impact of Control Technology*, 12(1):161–166, 2011.
7. Li Zhang, Wang Qing, and Tian Bin. Security threats and measures for the cyber-physical systems. *The Journal of China Universities of Posts and Telecommunications*, 20:25–29, 2013.
8. Abdulmalik Humayed, Jingqiang Lin, Fengjun Li, and Bo Luo. Cyber-physical systems security: A survey. *IEEE Internet of Things Journal*, 4(6):1802–1831, 2017.
9. Manish Snehi and Abhinav Bhandari. Vulnerability retrospection of security solutions for software-defined cyber–physical system against ddos and iot-ddos attacks. *Computer Science Review*, 40:100–371, 2021.
10. Jay Lee, Edzel Lapira, Shanhu Yang, and Ann Kao. Predictive manufacturing system-trends of next-generation production systems. *IFAC Proceedings Volumes*, 46(7):150–156, 2013.
11. Stefan Heng. Industry 4.0: Huge potential for value creation waiting to be tapped. Deutsche Bank Research, pages 8–10, 2014.
12. Bilal Hussain, Qinghe Du, Bo Sun, and Zhiqiang Han. Deep learning-based ddos-attack detection for cyber–physical system over 5g network. *IEEE Transactions on Industrial Informatics*, 17(2):860–870, 2020.
13. Constantinos Kolias, Georgios Kambourakis, Angelos Stavrou, and Jeffrey Voas. Ddos in the iot: Mirai and other botnets. *Computer*, 50(7):80–84, 2017.
14. Rasim Alguliyev, Yadigar Imamverdiyev, and Lyudmila Sukhostat. Cyber-physical systems and their security issues. *Computers in Industry*, 100:212–223, 2018.
15. NIST. https://www.nist.gov/el/cyber-physical-systems, Nov 2019.
16. Edward A Lee. Computing foundations and practice for cyber-physical systems: A preliminary report. University of California, Berkeley, CA, *Tech. Rep. UCB/EECS-2007-72, 21*, 2007.
17. B Krogh, MD Ilic, and SS Sastry. Networked embedded control for cyber-physical systems: Research strategies and roadmap. *Technical Report*, 2007.
18. M Branicky. Cps initiative overview. In Proceedings of the IEEE/RSJ International Conference on Robotics and Cyber-Physical Systems. IEEE, 2008.
19. MA Wenfang. Cps: Sensor-net to sensor-acuator-net. *China Information World*, 25(41):310–315, 2010.
20. Edward A Lee. Cyber physical systems: Design challenges. In 2008 11th IEEE International Symposium on Object and Component-oriented Real-time Distributed Computing (ISORC), pages 363–369. IEEE, Orlando, FL, 2008.
21. He Jifeng. Cyber-physical systems. *Communications of the China Computer Federation*, 6(1):25–29, 2010.
22. Hyun Jung La and Soo Dong Kim. A service-based approach to designing cyber physical systems. In 2010 IEEE/ACIS 9th International Conference on

Computer and Information Science, pages 895–900. IEEE, Vancouver, Canada, 2010.

23. BX Huang. Cyber physical systems: A survey. *Presentation Report,* Jun, 2008.

24. Bruce H Krogh. Cyber physical systems: The need for new models and design paradigms. *Presentation Report,* 2008.

25. JZ Li, H Gao, and B Yu. Concepts, features, challenges, and research progresses of cpss. *Development Report of China Computer Science,* pages 1–17, 2009.

26. Raj Rajkumar. *Cps Briefing.* Carnegie Mellon University, 2007.

27. Sajal Bhatia, Sunny Behal, and Irfan Ahmed. Distributed denial of service attacks and defense mechanisms: Current landscape and future directions. In *Versatile Cybersecurity,* pages 55–97. Springer, 2018.

28. Liwei An and Guang-Hong Yang. Improved adaptive resilient control against sensor and actuator attacks. *Information Sciences,* 423:145–156, 2018.

29. Shamsul Huda, Suruz Miah, Mohammad Mehedi Hassan, Rafiqul Islam, John Yearwood, Majed Alrubaian, and Ahmad Almogren. Defending unknown attacks on cyber-physical systems by semi-supervised approach and available unlabeled data. *Information Sciences,* 379:211–228, 2017.

30. Xu Jin, Wassim M Haddad, and Tansel Yucelen. An adaptive control architecture for mitigating sensor and actuator attacks in cyber-physical systems. *IEEE Transactions on Automatic Control,* 62(11):6058–6064, 2017.

31. An-Yang Lu and Guang-Hong Yang. Event-triggered secure observer-based control for cyber-physical systems under adversarial attacks. *Information Sciences,* 420:96–109, 2017.

32. An-Yang Lu and Guang-Hong Yang. Secure state estimation for cyber-physical systems under sparse sensor attacks via a switched luenberger observer. *Information Sciences,* 417:454–464, 2017.

33. Robert Mitchell and Ray Chen. Modeling and analysis of attacks and counter defense mechanisms for cyber physical systems. *IEEE Transactions on Reliability,* 65(1):350–358, 2015.

34. Yasser Shoukry, Pierluigi Nuzzo, Alberto Puggelli, Alberto L Sangiovanni-Vincentelli, Sanjit A Seshia, and Paulo Tabuada. Secure state estimation for cyber-physical systems under sensor attacks: A satisfiability modulo theory approach. *IEEE Transactions on Automatic Control,* 62(10):4917–4932, 2017.

35. Richard Poisel. *Modern Communications Jamming Principles and Techniques.* Artech House, 2011.

36. Chee-Wooi Ten, Govindarasu Manimaran, and Chen-Ching Liu. Cybersecurity for critical infrastructures: Attack and defense modeling. *IEEE Transactions on Systems, Man, and Cybernetics-Part A: Systems and Humans,* 40(4):853–865, 2010.

37. Crispin Cowan, Steve Beattie, John Johansen, and Perry Wagle. Pointguardtm: Protecting pointers from buffer overflow vulnerabilities. In Proceedings of the 12th conference on USENIX Security Symposium, volume 12, pages 91–104, Washington, DC, 2003.

38. Hovav Shacham, Matthew Page, Ben Pfaff, Eu-Jin Goh, Nagendra Modadugu, and Dan Boneh. On the effectiveness of address-space randomization. In Proceedings of the 11th ACM Conference on Computer and Communications Security, pages 298–307, Washington, DC, 2004.

39. Dayu Yang, Alexander Usynin, and J Wesley Hines. Anomaly-based intrusion detection for scada systems. In 5th International Topical Meeting on Nuclear

Plant Instrumentation, Control and Human Machine Interface Technologies (NPIC&HMIT 05), pages 12–16, 2006.

40. Steven Cheung, Bruno Dutertre, Martin Fong, Ulf Lindqvist, Keith Skinner, and Alfonso Valdes. Using model-based intrusion detection for scada networks. In Proceedings of the SCADA Security Scientific Symposium, volume 46, pages 1–12. Citeseer, Belfast, UK, 2007.

41. Saurabh Amin, Alvaro A Cardenas, and S Shankar Sastry. Safe and secure networked control systems under denial-of-service attacks. In International Workshop on Hybrid Systems: Computation and Control, pages 31–45. Springer, San Francisco, CA, 2009.

42. Christopher Zimmer, Balasubramanya Bhat, Frank Mueller, and Sibin Mohan. Time-based intrusion detection in cyber-physical systems. In Proceedings of the 1st ACM/IEEE International Conference on Cyber-Physical Systems, pages 109–118, Stockholm, Sweden, 2010.

43. Upeka Kanchana Premaratne, Jagath Samarabandu, Tarlochan S Sidhu, Robert Beresh, and Jian-Cheng Tan. An intrusion detection system for iec61850 automated substations. IEEE Transactions on Power Delivery, 25(4):2376–2383, 2010.

44. Wei Gao, Thomas Morris, Bradley Reaves, and Drew Richey. On scada control system command and response injection and intrusion detection. In 2010 eCrime Researchers Summit, pages 1–9. IEEE, 2010.

45. Yuan Yuan, Quanyan Zhu, Fuchun Sun, Qinyi Wang, and Tamer Baffsar. Resilient control of cyber-physical systems against denial-of-service attacks. In 2013 6th International Symposium on Resilient Control Systems (ISRCS), pages 54–59. IEEE, 2013.

46. Minghui Zhu and Sonia Martjnez. On distributed constrained formation control in operator–vehicle adversarial networks. Automatica, 49(12):3571–3582, 2013.

47. Lei Su and Dan Ye. A cooperative detection and compensation mechanism against denial-of-service attack for cyber-physical systems. Information Sciences, 444:122–134, 2018.

7

SS-DDoS: Spark-Based DDoS Attacks Classification Approach

Nilesh Vishwasrao Patil, C. Rama Krishna and Krishan Kumar

CONTENTS

7.1 Introduction

In this era, there is exponential growth in communication technologies. Therefore, there is a massive growth in data communication between clients and web-based applications. Every sector of organizations, such as financial, academics, transport, and human resources, deploys its online systems on several web servers for availability anytime to clients. However, this impressive growth attracts attackers to launch attacks on the victim system. A Distributed Denial of Service (DDoS) is one of the massive threats to web-based systems. It immediately devastates the resources of web-based systems by transferring large numbers of network packets. Therefore, it denies access to genuine clients [1]. It can be launched by compromising large numbers of devices, such as IoT devices, smartphones, and computers, and transferring large numbers of irrelevant packets in a coordinated manner. Therefore, the critical challenge is to classify incoming network traces with a better classification rate and real-time replies. In the literature, several techniques have been proposed to protect web-based systems from different types of attacks.

DOI: 10.1201/9781003185543-7

However, occurrences of attacks are increasing year after year. Therefore, there is a need to provide a real-time and distributed classification approach for classifying incoming network traces into two classes: benign and DDoS attacks.

In today's big data environment, the traditional framework-based classification approaches need more time for the analysis of large numbers of network packets. Therefore, it is necessary to design and deploy the proposed distributed classification model on distributed big data processing frameworks, such as Apache Spark Streaming [2]. Furthermore, in the literature, few techniques are employed to design machine learning-based models, such as python, R, Java, and WEKA. However, they faced scalability issues after deploying the designed model on distributed frameworks. Therefore, there is a need to design machine learning-based classification models using distributed libraries, such as Spark MLlib on the Hadoop cluster.

The following are the notable contributions in this chapter:

- Proposed a distributed and real-time Spark Streaming-based classification approach for DDoS attacks, named SS-DDoS.
- SS-DDoS distributes the computational cost among several machines.
- SS-DDoS efficiently classifies incoming network traces into two classes: DDoS attacks and benign.
- SS-DDoS operates in an automated mode as Spark Streaming consumes incoming network packets from sinks and classifies them immediately into two classes.
- The proposed distributed classification model provides a highly scalable feature as being designed using distributed machine learning algorithms.

This chapter is organized as follows. Section 7.2 analyzes existing distributed classification techniques. Section 7.3 presents the proposed SS-DDoS classification approach, Section 7.4 presents the testbed information, while Section 7.5 provides the results and discussion of the SS-DDoS. Finally, Section 7.6 concludes this chapter.

7.2 Related Work

In the literature, numerous approaches have been proposed by researchers to protect web-based systems from different types of DDoS attacks. Patil et al. [3] systematically categorized existing classification approaches broadly into two classes: traditional and distributed processing frameworks. In this chapter, our primary focus is on distributed framework-based DDoS

TABLE 7.1

Summary of distributed frameworks-based classification approaches for DDoS attacks

Authors	Testbed details	Methodology
Lee and Lee [4]	01+10 [Namenode+Datanodes] Configuration: Intel-i7, HDD:1TB, RAM:16GB	Parameter: Access pattern, Timestamp, Detection metrics: Time interval, threshold, and unbalanced ratio
Khattak et al. [5]	Karmasphere (environment), for Hadoop cluster	Horizontal (number of requests on victims) and vertical (number of requests on victim network)
Zhao et al. [6]	01 Apache Server, Hadoop cluster: 01 + 02 [Namenode+Datanodes]	Parameters: Avg. CPU Usage, packet size, and number of TCP connections
Dayama et al. [7]	01 + 10 [Namenode + Datanodes], Configuration: Intel-i7, HDD: 1TB, RAM: 16GB.	Number of incoming request from specific clients
Hameed et al. [8]	01+01+10 [Capturing node+Namenode+Datanodes], Configuration: Intel core-i5, RAM: 8GB, HDD: 500GB	Parameters: Timestamp, Source IP, No. of requests from particular Source IP [Th = 500/1,000]
Chhabra et al. [9]	Hadoop-2.7.1 cluster: 01+04 [Namenode+Datanodes],	Algorithm: Random Forest based Decision Tree
Patil et al. [10]	Hadoop Cluster: 01+30 [Namenode+Datanodes]	Shannon-Entropy
Vani et al. [11]	Intel i5/core-i7, CPU-3.20GHz, RAM-4GB	Parameters: Flow duration, protocol, src-bytes, dst-bytes, flag, Detection metrics: Source IP entropy
Patil et al. [12]	Hadoop Cluster: 01+03 [Namenode+Datanodes]	Detection metrics: Source IP entropy

classification approaches. Few researchers proposed distributed framework-based classification systems. However, several approaches are tested in offline mode. In Table 7.1, we summarize distributed framework-based classification approaches.

7.3 Proposed SS-DDoS Classification Approach for DDoS Attacks

In this section, we present the comprehensive workflow of the SS-DDoS. The logical architecture of the proposed SS-DDoS classification approach is shown in Figure 7.1. We design a distributed classification model using Spark MLlib K-Means clustering algorithm on the Hadoop cluster by fetching designing instances from HDFS. For this use case, we consider two clusters ($k = 2$): (i) DDoS attacks and (ii) Benign traces. As per our prior work \cite{patil2020s}, we extracted various network traffic parameters from

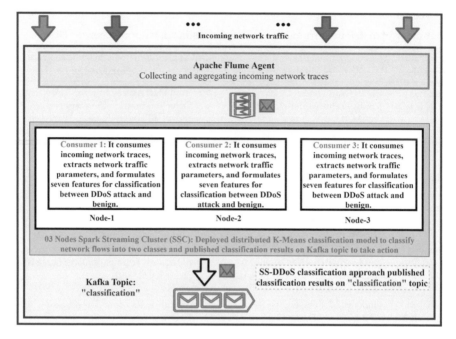

FIGURE 7.1
Logical architecture of the proposed SS-DDoS.

raw packets and formulated the seven most significant features based on using Shannon entropy (Sh_E), mean (Mn), and standard deviation (SD) from extracted parameters. These formulated features are used to design the proposed distributed classification approach.

- *Time Window*: The biggest challenge while designing a classification model for DDoS attacks is to choose the best $time_{window}$. The incorrect selection of $time_{window}$ affects the classification accuracy. For designing this distributed classification model, we select $time_{window}$ = 1 sec.

- *Network Traffic Parameters*: We extracted a few network traffic parameters from incoming raw packets, such as "source and destination IPs, source and destination port numbers, packet length, etc."

- Formulate features: For designing the proposed distributed classification model, we formulated the seven most significant features based on extracted network traffic attributes using statistical approaches Sh_E Mn and SD in the $time_{window}$. In Table 7.2, we summarize each feature.

- Preprocessing: The next step for designing the proposed distributed classification model is to perform preprocessing task on formulated features. Few features have a different range of values; therefore, there is a need to normalize each formulated feature on the same

TABLE 7.2

Formulated features for designing distributed classification model

Feature	Summary
Feature 1	Number of incoming requests in the $time_{window}$
Feature 2	Mn of requests per source IP in the $time_{window}$
Feature 3	SD of incoming requests per source IP in the $time_{window}$
Feature 4	Sh_E of source IP distribution in the $time_{window}$
Feature 5	Mn of entropy contribution per source IP in the $time_{window}$
Feature 6	SD of entropy contribution per source IP in the $time_{window}$
Feature 7	Avg. length of incoming requests in the $time_{window}$

scale. It will help to improve the classification accuracy of the proposed classification model. Few libraries have been provided to normalize data; in this use case, we employ *PySpark* and *PySparkling* normalization library.

We classify the proposed distributed classification model into two steps: (i) the distributed designing process of the classification model on the Hadoop cluster and (ii) the deployment of the designed model on the Spark Streaming cluster.

7.3.1 Designing Process of the Proposed Distributed Classification Model

The comprehensive designing process of the proposed distributed classification model for DDoS attacks and Benign traces is presented in Figure 7.2. The prime purpose of this distributed classification model is to classify incoming raw packets into two classes: DDoS attacks and Benign traces. We design this distributed classification model using the Spark MLlib K-Means clustering algorithm on the Hadoop cluster. After designing this model, we stored it in persistent storage for deploying it on the Spark Streaming cluster.

For designing this model, we generated synthetic network traces and captured them using the designed testbed. We considered the sampling time to be 800 seconds (*ST*) and stored the captured raw packets in HDFS. We extracted a few network traffic parameters and formulated features (presented in Table 7.2) based on them. After that, we employed the Spark MLlib K-Means clustering algorithm and evaluated the performance of the model. Finally, we saved this model to deploy on the Spark Streaming cluster.

7.3.2 Deployment of the Designed Model on the Spark Streaming Cluster

The comprehensive deployment process of the proposed distributed classification model is presented in Figure 7.3 for classifying incoming raw packets

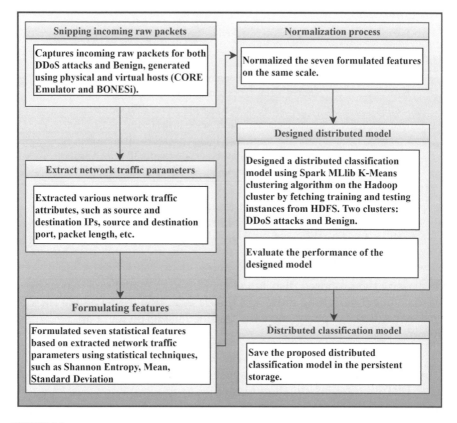

FIGURE 7.2
Designing process of the proposed distributed classification model for DDoS attacks and benign traces on the Hadoop cluster.

into two classes and publishing results on the Kafka topic. The prime purpose of this step is to classify incoming raw packets in real time.

7.4 Experimental Set-up

In this section, we present the testbed details of the proposed SS-DDoS classification approach. We implemented a testbed to design and test the SS-DDoS, which is shown in Figure 7.4. The testbed includes physical and virtual hosts with the help of the CORE emulator and BoNeSi. The detail of the implemented testbed is given in the following:

- *One Machine*: For collecting incoming network traces and putting them into a sink with the help of Apache Flume.

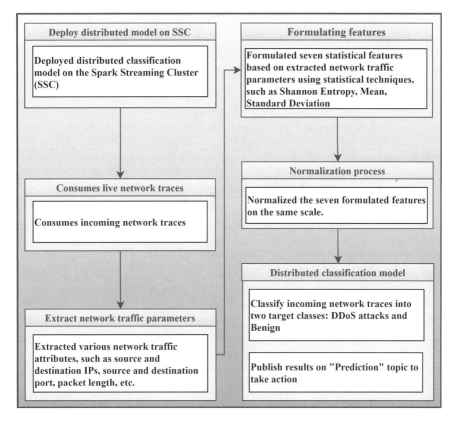

FIGURE 7.3
Classifying incoming network traces into two classes and publishes results on the Kafka topic (after deploying on SSC).

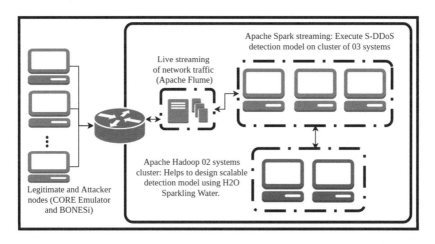

FIGURE 7.4
The implemented testbed for the proposed SS-DDoS classification approach.

- *Three Machines*: Implemented SSC for deploying the proposed distributed classification approach.
- *02 Machines*: Implemented Apache Hadoop cluster to design the distributed classification model using Spark MLlib library.
- *02 Machines*: Used to generate synthetic network traces using the CORE.

7.5 Results and Discussion

In this section, we evaluate the performance of the SS-DDoS classification approach. To design and validate the proposed SS-DDoS, we generated synthetic network traces using physical and virtual machines. The proposed SS-DDoS classification approach consumes incoming network raw packets, analyzes them, and shares the workload between three machines of SSC. The primary objective of this approach is to identify DDoS attacks from incoming network traces in real time.

To evaluate the performance, we consider two scenarios: Scenario 1: during designing a distributed classification model on the Hadoop cluster and Scenario 2: after deploying the designed model on the SSC. We employed several performance metrics presented in [3, 10]. The evaluation for Scenario 1 and Scenario 2 is given in Table 7.3.

For Scenario 1, we collect and save incoming network traces into the HDFS. It is generated using the implemented testbed for approximately 800 seconds (*ST*). For the first 400 seconds, we generated legitimate and the next 400 seconds DDoS attack traces using the BoNeSi tool. Furthermore, the distributed classification model is designed using this generated data and validated using generating new data.

TABLE 7.3

Performance evaluation of the proposed distributed classification approach

Scenario	Sampling time	No. of packets	Precision	Recall	Accuracy
Scenario I (Designed data)	800	4,032,876	0.97	0.99	0.98
Scenario II	100	1,200,771	0.97	0.98	0.97
	200	2,401,452	0.98	0.98	0.98
	400	4,802,927	0.98	0.98	0.98

Scenario 1: During designing the proposed distributed classification model on the Hadoop Cluster.

Scenario 2: After deploying the designed distributed classification model on Spark Streaming Cluster.

For Scenario 2: Traced three cases based on different sampling time, such as (i) 100 seconds, (ii) 200 seconds, and (iii) 400 seconds.

TABLE 7.4

Comparison of the distributed SS-DDoS with existing approaches

Ref. No.	Deployed on	Deployment	Real-time
Lee and Lee [4]	Hadoop	Victim end	✗
Khattak [5]	Hadoop	Victim end	✗
Dayama et al. [7]	Hadoop	Victim end	✗
Hameed et al. [8, 14]	Hadoop	Victim end	✗
Maheshwari et al. [15]	Hadoop	Victim end	✗
Chhabra et al. [9]	Hadoop	Victim end	✗
Patil et al. [10]	Hadoop	ISP level	✗
SS-DDoS (Proposed)	Spark Streaming, Hadoop	Victim end	✓

In Table 7.4, we compared our proposed distributed approach with existing distributed approaches. In [4–10, 12–15], several distributed approaches are available. However, most of the existing approaches are designed and validated in offline mode, and, therefore, they failed to analyze incoming network traces in real-time mode.

7.6 Conclusions

A DDoS attack is a critical threat to web-based systems and overwhelms systems by transferring a large number of attack packets. Several classification approaches have been proposed in the literature to provide solutions for web-based systems from different kinds of DDoS attacks. However, DDoS attacks occurrences are growing year after year. In this chapter, we proposed Spark Streaming-based DDoS classification approach named SS-DDoS. It is designed using the distributed Spark MLlib by employing the K-Means clustering algorithm. After that, deployed the distributed K-Means clustering-based classification model on the Spark Streaming Cluster. The proposed SS-DDoS efficiently classifies incoming network traces in real time with 98% classification accuracy. In the future, we will design distributed classification model using the recent CICDDoS2019 data set and classify them into multiple classes, such as DDoS-DNS, DDoS-UDP, and DDoS-SYN.

References

1. Monika Sachdeva and Krishan Kumar. 'A traffic cluster entropy based approach to distinguish ddos attacks from ash event using deter testbed'. *ISRN Communications and Networking*, 2014:1–15, 2014.

2. Apache Spark. https://spark.apache.org/, 2021.
3. Nilesh Vishwasrao Patil, C Rama Krishna, and Krishan Kumar. 'Distributed frameworks for detecting distributed denial of service attacks: A comprehensive review, challenges and future directions'. *Concurrency and Computation: Practice and Experience*, 33(10):e6197, 2021.
4. Yeonhee Lee and Youngseok Lee. 'Detecting DDoS attacks with Hadoop'. In Proceedings of The ACM CoNEXT Student Workshop, page 7. ACM, Tokyo, Japan, 2011.
5. Rana Khattak, Shehar Bano, Shujaat Hussain, and Zahid Anwar. 'Dofur: DDoS forensics using Mapreduce'. In *Frontiers of Information Technology (FIT)*, 2011, pages 117–120. IEEE, 2011.
6. Teng Zhao, Dan Chia-Tien Lo, and Kai Qian. 'A neural-network based ddos detection system using Hadoop and Hbase'. In 2015 IEEE 17th International Conference on High Performance Computing and Communications (HPCC), 2015 IEEE 7th International Symposium on Cyberspace Safety and Security (CSS), 2015 IEEE 12th International Conference on Embedded Software and Systems (ICESS), pages 1326–1331. IEEE, New York, 2015.
7. RS Dayama, Aakanksh Bhandare, Bhagayshri Ganji, and Vijaya Narayankar. 'Secured network from distributed DoS through hadoop'. *International Journal of Computer Applications*, 118(2):20–22, 2015.
8. Suffan Hameed and Usman Ali. 'Hadec: Hadoop-based live DDoS detection framework'. *EURASIP Journal on Information Security*, 2018(1):1–19, 2018.
9. Gurpal Singh Chhabra, Varinderpal Singh, and Maninder Singh. 'Hadoop-based analytic framework for cyber forensics'. *International Journal of Communication Systems*, Wiley Online Library, 31(15):e3772, 2018.
10. Nilesh Vishwasrao Patil, C Rama Krishna, Krishan Kumar, and Sunny Behal. 'E-had: A distributed and collaborative detection framework for early detection of DDoS attacks'. *Journal of King Saud University-Computer and Information Sciences*, 2019.
11. YK Vani and P Ranjana. 'Detection of distributed denial of service attack using dlmn algorithm in Hadoop'. *Journal of Critical Review*, 7(11):1011–1017, 2020.
12. Nilesh Vishwasrao Patil, C Rama Krishna, and Krishan Kumar. 'Apache Hadoop based distributed denial of service detection framework'. In International Conference on Information, Communication and Computing Technology, pages 25–35. Springer, 2019.
13. Nilesh Vishwasrao Patil, C Rama Krishna, and Krishan Kumar. 'S-DDoS: Apache spark based real-time ddos detection system. *Journal of Intelligent & Fuzzy Systems*, 8(5):6527–6535, 2020.
14. Suffan Hameed and Usman Ali. 'Efficacy of live DDoS detection with hadoop'. In Network Operations and Management Symposium (NOMS), 2016 IEEE/IFIP, pages 488–494. IEEE, Istanbul, Turkey, 2016.
15. Vishal Maheshwari, Ashutosh Bhatia, and Kuldeep Kumar. 'Faster detection and prediction of ddos attacks using mapreduce and time series analysis'. In 2018 International Conference on Information Networking (ICOIN), pages 556–561. IEEE, Chiang Mai, 2018.

8

Mininet-WiFi as Software-Defined Wireless Network Testing Platform

Karamjeet Kaur, Sukhveer Kaur, Krishan Kumar,
Naveen Aggarwal and Veenu Mangat

CONTENTS

8.1 Introduction

To increase internet connectivity across the world, deploying a wireless network at a very large scale is one of the major steps because a wired network is very difficult to manage at a large scale. In a traditional network, deployment of wireless LAN at a very large scale is a very tedious task because we have to manage thousands of access points that are deployed in the wireless network. It is an error-prone task to configure each and every device separately [1]. Moreover, intercommunication is mandatory to balance the load among the number of APs. This means it is necessary to get the information about the current position of the wireless LAN so the necessary changes can be made. A centralized management scheme is one of the solutions to address this problem. All the access points communicate with the central device called controller that manages the whole network from the central location. The centralized management of these wireless devices raises interoperability issues because all devices are made by different manufacturers with different standards. To address this issue, different vendor access points must be managed in a standard manner by a single controller.

Software Defined Network (SDN) is a new network paradigm that restructures the network by separating the data plane and control plane [2]. This

DOI: 10.1201/9781003185543-8

architecture has a lot of benefits. First, it reduces the load on the wireless equipment and shifts it to the centralized controller. Second, it reduces the network cost due to the separation of both planes. Furthermore, it presents the global view of the whole network to the network administrator. The wired network uses the SDN architecture at a very large scale to control the flow and routing among the devices such as OpenFlow-enabled devices. In this scenario, the central controller uses the OpenFlow protocol to modify the flow rules into the flow table of the switch. SDN is also used for easy and efficient management of wireless LAN. It helps to remove the processing load at the access points, enables central management of the whole network, and reduce the cost of access points. This architecture is also known as Software Defined Wireless Network (SDWN) [3].

The remaining part of this chapter is organized as follows. Section 8.2 discusses SDWN and protocols used in wireless LAN. Section 8.3 gives detailed information about emulation tools for a wireless network, that is, Mininet-WiFi. It is basically an extension of Mininet that is used in wired SDN networks. Different topologies are also discussed in this section. Section 8.4 gives a bird's eye view of how we can create custom topologies using python scripts. Section 8.5 describes the conclusion of the whole scenario.

8.2 Software Defined Wireless Network

Software Defined Networking is a new paradigm in the field of networking that separates the data plane and control plane [4]. As both planes are separated from each other, OpenFlow protocol [5, 6] is used for communication between the data plane (OpenFlow-enabled devices) and the control plane (SDN controller). In a similar manner, Software Defined Wireless Network (SDWN) [7] is used to manage the whole wireless network (consists of access points) from the central location. The OpenFlow protocol that we used in a wired network is not suitable for a wireless network as it cannot satisfy needs such as mobility and channel selection according to the movement. The Open Network Foundation (ONF) [8] may change this architecture in the near future. But now, the best approach to using WiFi and OpenFlow together is the "OpenWRT" [9] firmware that is open-source OS. This open-source firmware helps to turn the traditional wireless router into OpenFlow-enabled device.

The various components of SDWN are shown in Figure 8.1. In this architecture, two hosts, h1 and h2, are created with the original Mininet approach having interface "h1-etho" with the access point interface "ap1-eth1" and "h2-eth0" with the access point interface "ap1-eth2". There are also newly created wireless devices such as sta1 (having interface sta1-wlan0) and sta2 (having interface sta2-wlan0) connected with the WiFi interface of AP such as "ap1-wlan1".

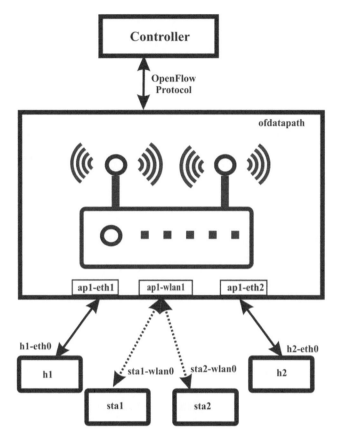

FIGURE 8.1
SDWN architecture.

There are two standard protocols used to manage the wireless network: CAPWAP (Control and Provisioning of Wireless Access Points) and TR069 (Technical Report 069) [10]. In a wireless LAN, these protocols are used for communication between a controller and wireless equipment. These protocols act as a southbound interface.

8.3 Mininet-WiFi

Mininet-WiFi is an emulator tool that is used as a testing platform for software-defined wireless networks. Mininet-WiFi is an extension of the Mininet emulator [11]. The developers of Mininet-WiFi [12] did not modify the existing functionality but only added the new features to the existing Mininet. The mobility functions and WiFi interfaces are the two functionalities that are added by the Mininet-WiFi into Mininet. Both functionalities are based on "wireless Linux driver" and "80211_hwsim wireless simulation driver". There are several default topologies, including minimal, single, and linear, which are similar to Mininet with the exception that the switch works as a wireless access point. The hosts act like a wireless station. In each topology, the wireless station is connected to the access point through an "ap1-wlan1" interface. In general, each station is connected with an access point using infrastructure mode, which means that whenever a wireless station wants to communicate with the other station, traffic must pass through the wireless access point. Station 1 has an interface "sta1-wlan0", and station 2 has an interface "sta2-wlan0", and so on. Access point numbering starts from 1. In the following section, we discuss the Mininet-WiFi installation steps, Mininet-WiFi default topologies, and custom topologies that are created with the help of Python API.

- Mininet-WiFi installation
- Mininet-WiFi default topologies
- Mininet-WiFi custom topologies

8.3.1　Mininet-WiFi Installation

Step 1: Install Ubuntu 16.04 virtual machine on a Virtual Box virtualization software because it is open source.

Step 2: Configure this Ubuntu virtual machine and set the IP address "172.24.0.61".

Step 3: To install Mininet-WiFi, the following four steps are performed:

- "sudo apt-get update"
- "sudo apt-get install git"
- "git clone https://github.com/intrig-unicamp/mininet-wifi"
- "cd mininet-wifi"
- sudo util/install.sh -Wnf3vpw (W to install dependencies, n to install core files, f to install Openflow, 3 means OpenFlow version 1.3, v means install openvswitch, p to install POX, w to install wireshark)

8.3.2　Mininet-WiFi Default Topologies

- *Minimal Topology*: This is a basic topology consisting of one wireless access point having interface "ap1-wlan1", which is connected to two wireless stations having interfaces "sta1-wlan0" and "sta2-wlan0", as shown in Figure 8.2.

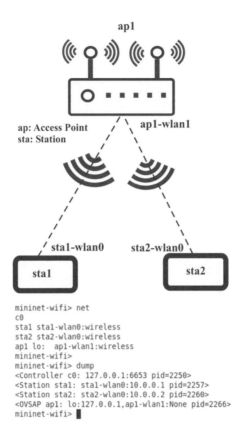

```
mininet-wifi> net
c0
sta1 sta1-wlan0:wireless
sta2 sta2-wlan0:wireless
ap1 lo:  ap1-wlan1:wireless
mininet-wifi>
mininet-wifi> dump
<Controller c0: 127.0.0.1:6653 pid=2250>
<Station sta1: sta1-wlan0:10.0.0.1 pid=2257>
<Station sta2: sta2-wlan0:10.0.0.2 pid=2260>
<OVSAP ap1: lo:127.0.0.1,ap1-wlan1:None pid=2266>
mininet-wifi> █
```

FIGURE 8.2
Minimal topology.

- *Single Topology*: In a single topology, one access point is connected to k number of wireless stations. In our case, the value of k is 4, meaning that four wireless stations, such as sta1, sta2, sta3, and sta4, having interface "sta1-wlan0", "sta2-wlan0", "sta3-wlan0", and "sta4-wlan0" are connected to a wireless access point having interface "ap1-wlan1" (Figure 8.3).

mn –wifi - topo single, 4

- *Linear Topology*: This topology consists of k wireless access points and k wireless stations. Each wireless station is connected to the corresponding access point through a wireless interface. This topology also creates a link between each access point through physical Ethernet card (Figure 8.4).

mn –wifi –topo linear, 4

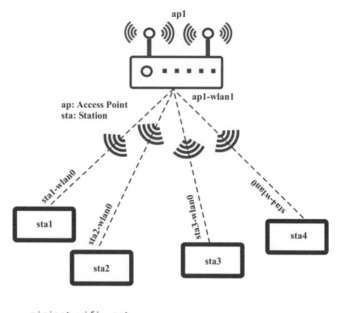

```
mininet-wifi> net
c0
sta1 sta1-wlan0:wireless
sta2 sta2-wlan0:wireless
sta3 sta3-wlan0:wireless
sta4 sta4-wlan0:wireless
ap1 lo:  ap1-wlan1:wireless
mininet-wifi>
mininet-wifi> dump
<Controller c0: 127.0.0.1:6653 pid=2691>
<Station sta1: sta1-wlan0:10.0.0.1 pid=2698>
<Station sta2: sta2-wlan0:10.0.0.2 pid=2701>
<Station sta3: sta3-wlan0:10.0.0.3 pid=2704>
<Station sta4: sta4-wlan0:10.0.0.4 pid=2707>
<OVSAP ap1: lo:127.0.0.1,ap1-wlan1:None pid=2713>
mininet-wifi> █
```

FIGURE 8.3
Single topology.

Net and dump commands are used to check the connections between network nodes. In a linear topology, all the access points, such as ap1, ap2, ap3, and ap4, are connected using Ethernet links, but it is not clear which wireless station is connected to which access point. "iw scan" command is used to check the visible access point to each wireless station. Run this command on every wireless station. "iw link" command is used to check to which access point each station is connected. Also run this command on every wireless station.

"sta1 iw dev sta1-wlan0 scan | grep ssid"
"sta1 iw dev sta1-wlan0 link"

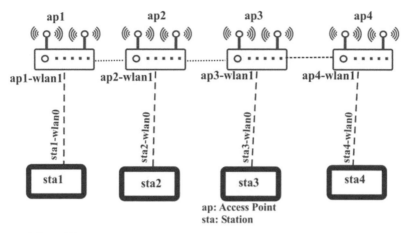

FIGURE 8.4
Linear topology.

For example, in Figure 8.5, all access points having SSIDs "ssid_ap1", "ssid_ap2", "ssid_ap3", and "ssid_ap4" are visible to sta1, but sta1 is currently connected to access point 1.

8.4 Mininet-WiFi Custom Topologies

The python API is available in Mininet to create custom topologies. To support a wireless environment, these APIs are extended in Mininet-WiFi. When we run an "mn" command with –wifi option, we do not access most of the functionality of Mininet-WiFi. To use the proper features of Mininet-WiFi in

```
mininet-wifi> sta1 iw dev sta1-wlan0 scan |grep ssid
        SSID: ssid_ap1
        SSID: ssid_ap2
        SSID: ssid_ap3
        SSID: ssid_ap4
mininet-wifi>
mininet-wifi> sta1 iw dev sta1-wlan0 link
Connected to 02:00:00:00:04:00 (on sta1-wlan0)
        SSID: ssid_ap1
        freq: 2412
        RX: 3122208 bytes (54761 packets)
        TX: 11147 bytes (234 packets)
        signal: -30 dBm
        tx bitrate: 54.0 MBit/s

        bss flags:      short-slot-time
        dtim period:    2
        beacon int:     100
mininet-wifi> ■
```

FIGURE 8.5
Check visible and connected access points.

a wireless environment, we have to use the Mininet-WiFi python API. The number of classes is added to python API that is used to emulate the network nodes in a wireless network. The addStation, addAccessPoint, and addLink are the methods that support the wireless network. Figure 8.6 shows a custom topology having two access points and five wireless stations. The major benefit of this method is that we can create a network according to our requirements.

The following command is used to run the custom topology that consists of two access points and five wireless stations.

"python custom-topo.py"

The following functions are used to create a custom topology:

- addStation ("name of station", "MACaddress", "IP address", "position"): For station1, we are passing parameters "sta1", "00:00:00:00:00:01", "172.24.0.1/16", and position is "30,60,0", which means that 30 meters in x direction, 60 in y direction, and 0 in z direction. This method is called five times for all other stations.
- addAccessPoint ("name of access point", "ssid", "position", "range"): For accesspoint1, we are passing parameters "ap1", "ap1", and position is "50,50,0", which means that 50 meters in x direction, 50 meters in y direction, and 0 in z direction. We specify the range = 50, which specifies the area of the access point. This method is called two times for both the access points.

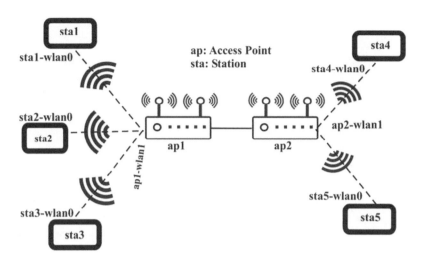

FIGURE 8.6
Custom topology.

- plotGraph (x, y): This method is a very important method for a WiFi network to see the positions of network nodes in space. It is a graphical representation of network nodes. We are passing 300,300 in x and y directions, respectively.
- addLink ("node1", "node2"): In this, we are passing parameters such as ap1 and ap2, which show an Ethernet wired connection between two access points.

Figure 8.7 shows that sta1, sta2, and sta3 are connected to ap1 through a wireless interface "ap1-wlan1". The other stations, such as sta4 and sta5, are connected to "ap2-wlan1".

Moreover, sta1 is able to communicate with sta3 as they are connected to the same access point. The station "sta2" is also able to communicate with "sta4", although both are connected to different access points (Figure 8.8). The reason is that we created an Ethernet connection between both access points.

The most important feature of Mininet-WiFi is mobility that allows wireless stations to move around the space. Mininet-WiFi adds new methods such as startMobility() and mobility() into the existing python library. For example, in our topology, we want that sta1 and sta5 exchange their positions with each other. The following parameters are passed to the mobility() functions.

"net.mobility(sta1, 'start', time=1, position='30,60,0')"

"net.mobility(sta1, 'stop', time=10, position='140,120,0')"

"net.mobility(sta5, 'start', time=1, position='140,1200,0')"

"net.mobility(sta5, 'stop', time=10, position='30,60,0')"

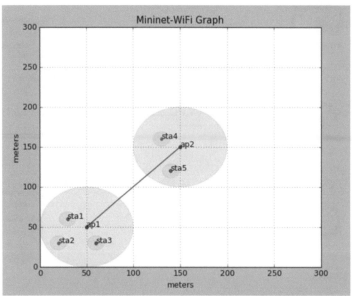

```
mininet-wifi> sta1 iw dev sta1-wlan0 link |grep SSID
        SSID: ap1
mininet-wifi> sta2 iw dev sta2-wlan0 link |grep SSID
        SSID: ap1
mininet-wifi> sta3 iw dev sta3-wlan0 link |grep SSID
        SSID: ap1
mininet-wifi> sta4 iw dev sta4-wlan0 link |grep SSID
        SSID: ap2
mininet-wifi> sta5 iw dev sta5-wlan0 link |grep SSID
        SSID: ap2
```

FIGURE 8.7
Before mobilty.py script running.

```
mininet-wifi> sta1 ping -c1 sta3
PING 172.24.0.3 (172.24.0.3) 56(84) bytes of data.
64 bytes from 172.24.0.3: icmp_seq=1 ttl=64 time=9.16 ms

--- 172.24.0.3 ping statistics ---
1 packets transmitted, 1 received, 0% packet loss, time 0ms
rtt min/avg/max/mdev = 9.162/9.162/9.162/0.000 ms
mininet-wifi> sta2 ping -c1 sta4
PING 172.24.0.4 (172.24.0.4) 56(84) bytes of data.
64 bytes from 172.24.0.4: icmp_seq=1 ttl=64 time=32.1 ms

--- 172.24.0.4 ping statistics ---
1 packets transmitted, 1 received, 0% packet loss, time 0ms
rtt min/avg/max/mdev = 32.147/32.147/32.147/0.000 ms
mininet-wifi> █
```

FIGURE 8.8
Network connectivity between wireless stations.

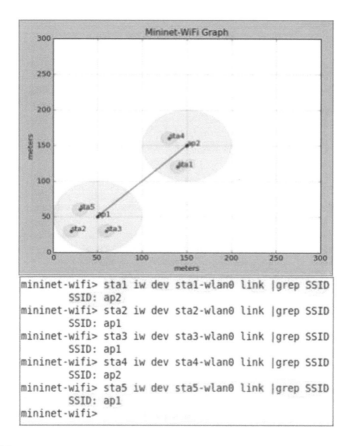

```
mininet-wifi> sta1 iw dev sta1-wlan0 link |grep SSID
        SSID: ap2
mininet-wifi> sta2 iw dev sta2-wlan0 link |grep SSID
        SSID: ap1
mininet-wifi> sta3 iw dev sta3-wlan0 link |grep SSID
        SSID: ap1
mininet-wifi> sta4 iw dev sta4-wlan0 link |grep SSID
        SSID: ap2
mininet-wifi> sta5 iw dev sta5-wlan0 link |grep SSID
        SSID: ap1
mininet-wifi>
```

FIGURE 8.9
After mobility.py script running.

As shown in Figure 8.9, sta1 and sta5 successfully move from one access point to another. Now sta5 is connected to ap1 as it is the nearest access point, and sta1 is connected to ap2 as it is the nearest access point.

8.5 Conclusion

Finally, we conclude that the decoupled architecture of SDN is highly beneficial for both wired and wireless networks. In addition, it makes network management easier with the help of a centralized controller. To experiment with SDWN, there are a number of options, such as testbeds, simulators, and emulators. Mininet-WiFi is an emulation tool that fulfills the needs of OpenFlow and WiFi experiments. Mininet-WiFi extends the functionality of Mininet by adding new functions and classes.

References

1. Yang, Mao, Yong Li, Depeng Jin, Lieguang Zeng, Xin Wu, and Athanasios V. Vasilakos. "Software-defined and virtualized future mobile and wireless networks: A survey." *Mobile Networks and Applications* 20, no. 1 (2015): 4–18.
2. Gupta, Vipin, Karamjeet Kaur, and Sukhveer Kaur. "Network programmability using software defined networking." In 2016 3rd International Conference on Computing for Sustainable Global Development (INDIACom), pp. 1170–1173. IEEE, New Delhi, 2016.
3. Abdelaziz Ahmed, Ang Tan Fong, Abdullah Gani, Suleman Khan, Faiz Alotaibi, and Muhammad Khurram Khan. "On software-defined wireless network (SDWN) network virtualization: Challenges and open issues." *The Computer Journal* 60, no. 10 (2017): 1510–1519.
4. Farhady, Hamid, HyunYong Lee, and Akihiro Nakao. "Software-defined networking: A survey." *Computer Networks* 81 (2015): 79–95.
5. McKeown, N., T. Anderson, and H. Balakrishnan. "OpenFlow: Enabling innovation in campus networks [J/OL]." *ACM Sigcomm Computer Communication Review* 38, no. 2 (2017): 69–74.
6. Zuo, Qing-Yun, Ming Chen, Guang-Song ZHAO, Chang-You XING, Guo-Min ZHANG, and Peicheng Jiang. "Research on OpenFlow-based SDN technologies." *Journal of Software* 5 (2013): 015.
7. Jagadeesan, Nachikethas A., and Bhaskar Krishnamachari. "Software-defined networking paradigms in wireless networks: A survey." *ACM Computing Surveys (CSUR)* 47, no. 2 (2015): 27.
8. https://www.opennetworking.org/sdn-resources/sdn-definition
9. https://openwrt.org/
10. Fontes, Ramon dos Reis, Mohamed Mahfoudi, Walid Dabbous, Thierry Turletti, and Christian Rothenberg. "How far can we go? towards realistic software-defined wireless networking experiments." *The Computer Journal* 60, no. 10 (2017): 1458–1471.
11. Kaur, Karamjeet, Japinder Singh, and Navtej Singh Ghumman. "Mininet as software defined networking testing platform." In International Conference on Communication, Computing & Systems (ICCCS), pp. 139–42. Firozpur, 2014.
12. Fontes, Ramon R., Samira Afzal, Samuel HB Brito, Mateus AS Santos, and Christian Esteve Rothenberg. "Mininet-WiFi: Emulating software-defined wireless networks." In 2015 11th International Conference on Network and Service Management (CNSM), pp. 384–389. IEEE, Barcelona, 2015.

9

Application of Cognitive Internet of Things (IoT) for COVID-19 Pandemic

Mayank Pathak, Dikchha Dwivedi, Navneet Kaur,
Vaibhav Chaturvedi, Anubhav Dwivedi, Ravi Pratap Singh,
Rajiv Kumar, Mahesh Patel and Hari Om Sharan

CONTENTS

9.1 Introduction

In this worldwide health epidemic, the medical industry is actively look-ing to track and control the dissemination of the COVID-19 pandemic (Coronavirus). IoT is one such technology area that can track the propaga-tion of the virus rapidly, recognize persons at high risk, and contain the virus in real time. They will also reliably assess the patient's prior diagnosis, the prevalence of long-term chronic diseases [1], to estimate the most likely mortality rate. Via group observation, health assistance, alerts, and disease prevention recommendations, IoT is a vital instrument to help us battle the current situation of COVID-19. The COVID-19 pandemic has infected all countries and significantly influenced clinical services and care programs. IoT is a well-established collection of advanced computational algorithms, computer, and electrical, mechanical, and physical systems with data transmission capacities across massive data networks, which largely overlook the need for any human interference. These instruments are all connected to their unique identifier numbers [2–6]. This specific technology serves as a gateway to techniques, data mining and patterns, philosophy of deep learning, sensory goods, etc. IoT is omnipresent in traditional tasks when physical devices work in multiple areas such as in-home protection systems and smart lighting systems, conveniently operated by voice-assisted smart speakers, smartphones, etc. In comparison, the IoT functionality suits our everyday needs.

In the current pandemic, all nations, including India, struggle with COVID-19 and are still finding a practical yet viable solution. Physical and engineering scientists are dedicated to solving these problems, developing new hypotheses, explaining new science concerns, providing user-centered descriptions, while also enlightening themselves and the whole civil community [7–9]. The short viewpoint would improve the awareness and core uses of this proprietary technology for COVID-19 disease outbreaks.

9.2 Context IoT Definition for the Epidemic of COVID-19

In 1982, the very first online appeal came into existence through the intent of distributing soda bottles, and Procter & Gamble coined the term IoT in 1999. Internet of things is intertwined systems and operations that are consistent with individual members of the structure, including some soft and hard network-backed access and any other elements of the network. Ultimately, the necessary electronics and quartans make them responsive by hosting the sharing and compilation of data. There are many technological areas in which the concept of IoT is well developed and efficient. These areas include consumer-related, industrial, infrastructure, and commercial applications. IoT has well-proven capabilities that establish the overall architectural context, which eventually enables the information between the service provider and service utilizer to be incorporated and efficiently shared. A large chunk of shortcomings that we face with this technology is due to the inadequate reachability of patients, which is the second most significant concern after the production of vaccines. The use of the IoT definition makes it very convenient for patients to be able to access them, which ultimately helps provide them with major therapy so that they can get out of this situation.

9.3 Need to Study

The rate of infection spread is rising globally at a steady rate in the troublesome current pandemic situation, and there is an immediate need to use the coordinated facilities provided by adopting the philosophical aspects of IoT. Also, IoT has already been used to support the purposes requested in various fields in which the existing problems are correlated with the IoHT (internet of healthcare things) or IoMT (internet of medical things). The current difficult situation with the COVID-19 is forcing medical professionals, employees, healthcare personnel, etc. to give their patients services and therapies in a more nuanced way - in an impactful, profitable, and efficient manner. This systematic analysis presents the potential means of providing orthopedic patients with medical treatment via the IoMT method during the COVID-19. In this pandemic, orthopedic patients often face several challenges, such as visiting treatment facilities, purchasing medicine, and testing and reporting results.

9.4 Important Role of IoT in COVID-19

The world has suffered at the start of 2020 with the latest dangerous respiratory syndrome. Coronavirus has sparked the pandemic intending to monitor the unexpected dissemination of the virus and the production of a vaccine. The need for comprehensive monitoring of people infected with COVID-19 is immense since most vaccine production attempts or involving COVID-19 propagation have not yet achieved adequate results. In recent years, IoT technology has earned tremendous interest in the health field. Social distancing is needed to deter this by installing IoT devices such as smart bands and multitude surveillance devices to monitor citizens in order to keep track of the necessary gap. Briefly, IoT technology has proven helpful since the COVID-19 pandemic in supporting patients, health practitioners, and officials. In this segment, we briefly identify the many gadgets and apps used mainly in the COVID-19 battle, such as wearables, helicopters, robots, IoT buttons, and mobile applications [10]. Table 9.1 summarizes the specifications of these systems in relation to this pandemic.

9.4.1 Wearables

Wearable devices may be defined as a mixture of electronics and anything that can be worn. These smart wearables have been built for different uses in various fields, including healthcare, fitness, and lifestyle. While data

TABLE 9.1

IoT-enabled technologies during COVID-19 [10]

S.No	Technology	Description	Pros	Cons
1.	Wearables	A mobile-assisted data receiving and analyzing technology that is worn on the body	Constant monitoring provides superior medicare Safe and efficient interface	Security and privacy of data Short battery life
2.	Drones	An uncrewed aerial vehicle with sensors and cameras, mapping system and communication systems	Human independent Accessible everywhere Omits inter-human interaction	Unprotected data transmission Requires maintenance
3.	Robots	A programmable machine that can manage complicated tasks such as living creatures	Safer and error resistant East to operate	Concerns about racism and privacy Reduce mental health problems
4.	Smartphones Apps	A software application designed to perform restricted tasks inside a mobile device	Monitoring and tracking	Collected data privacy, and security

protection remains to be an important problem with the proliferation of these applications, the market is expanding rapidly. IoT solutions provide a number of intelligent wearable technologies, including Digital Wearable, Smart Helmets, Smart Glasses, IoT-Q-Band, Easy Band, Google Lens, and Proximity Lens.

9.4.2 Drones

Drones are essentially aircraft that are flown without or with minimal human support by remote control. Various forms of IoT-based drones are used in the healthcare area and, in particular, in the war against COVID-19, including thermal imaging drones, disinfectant drones, surgical drones, tracking drones, advertisement drones, and multipurpose drones.

9.4.3 IoT Buttons

This type of IoT device is a small programmable button linked to the cloud through wireless communication. This computer will execute many routine tasks by pressing just one button based on its written cloud code. For example, a type of IoT button allows patients to complain about symptoms and works as a panic button.

9.4.4 Robots

The internet of robotic things (IoRT) was unveiled as an invention after the introduction of the networked robots inside the cloud, where many different activities can be carried out to improve existence. And in certain crucial circumstances, robotics play very important functions, including the cleanliness of specific covet centers and ensuring patients take medications at specified times. Robots should be categorized as distinct from the present pandemic - robots and social robots, interactive robots.

9.4.5 Smartphone Applications

Smartphone applications are mobile devices programmed inside a mobile system with minimal features, like a smartphone. These IoT smartphone applications can be highly effective in diverse sectors, such as healthcare, banking, and agriculture, as there were 3.5 billion operating smartphones by 2020. A range of mobile medical applications, including COVID-19 apps such as nCapp, Stop Corona, Social Tracking, Selfie app, Civitas, StayHomeSafe, AarogyaSetu, Trace Together, the alliance, study doors, WhatsApp and others have been created.

9.5 Hospital Digital Access during COVID-19 Pandemic Using IoT

The IoT strategy allows medical practitioners to leverage their network of resources and equipment for the care of patients. This included a well-systematically organized clinical development channel, a remote patient monitoring body, intelligent healthcare, data processing software, etc., many of which have a more effect on the internet operating systems that are so attractive such as wireless fidelity, Bluetooth, modems, etc. [11].

9.6 Avenues in IoT to Contain COVID-19

This technology is useful for storing and displaying data in real time and additional necessary details concerning the infected patient. Figure 9.1 illustrates the important processes used for COVID-19 by IoT. IoT, during the first stage, collected health data by tracing the footprints of an infected person and the various places they were in and using the virtual management system to analyze all the data. This technology allows the data to be monitored and the follow-up report to be achieved in a presentable format.

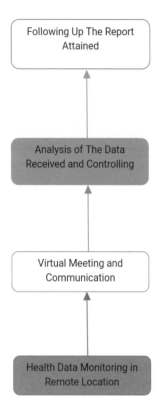

FIGURE 9.1
Step-up phase map for IoT implementation to combat the COVID-19 pandemic [7].

9.7 Possible Utilization of IoT for COVID-19 Pandemic

IoT utilizes a wide variety of user gadgets connecting to the same network to create a secure network with a sustainable health management system. To enhance the patient's protection, it monitors the patient and warns the hospital staff of any forms of complications. It gathers the patient's data and history sheet of past medical diagnoses digitally without any human contact. For suitable decision-making processes, this knowledge is also beneficial. The leading IoT applications for the COVID-19 pandemic are discussed in Table 9.2. For different applications, IoT is used to fulfill the essential requirements to mitigate the impact of the COVID-19 pandemic. It has the assistance of sufficient retrieved data from other hospital networks and from the patient recent diagnoses, which thereby gives it the ability to foresee any potential threats to the patient. In order to bring down the mortality rate in the absence of a vaccine, shared experience in handling some unforeseen/unprecedented symptoms for a particular age group or in general can

TABLE 9.2

Significant IoT for COVID-19 pandemic applications

S.No	Significant application	Description
1.	Internet-connected hospitals	To support a pandemic such as a coronavirus disease, a fully integrated network inside hospital premises is needed to deploy IoT
2.	Notify the staff during any emergency	This interconnected network would allow staff and patients, wherever possible, to respond quicker and more effectively
3.	Cost reduction	It is cost-effective since it is possible to avoid the expenses borne by patients during regular medical visits, testing, etc.
4.	The phase of automated treatment	The collection of treatment strategies is efficient and helps to manage cases adequately
5.	For the management of drugs	It is possible to measure the medication storage and consumption as IoT deals with the connected device channel throughout
6.	Network for wireless healthcare to recognize patients with COVID-19	It is possible to mount various genuine software on mobile phones, which renders identification much more efficient
7.	Rapid COVID-19 screening	The correct diagnosis will be attempted by smart linked care as the case received at the first instance. In the end, this makes screening much more efficient
8.	For health insurance companies	To avoid any potential fraud, the insured person can be monitored. This makes the statements and services more transparent
9.	Accurate forecasting of virus	Using specific statistical methods can also help forecast the situation in the coming years based on the available data study times. It would also help to prepare for a healthier working environment for the government, doctors, academicians, etc.

indeed turn out to be quite helpful [12–15]. The patient can use IoT services for careful supervision of pulse rate, heart rate, blood glucose meter, and other personalized treatment activities. It helps, especially with the treatment of the more fragile sect of the human populace, such as the elderly, as they are more prone to an ever-evolving virus that impacts the respiratory system like COVID-19.

9.8 Different Challenges and Future Scope of the Study

In this global pandemic case, the primary point of concern when using the IoT COVID-19 is the protection of the collected data, which is a specific form

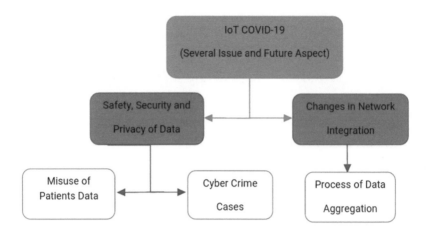

FIGURE 9.2
Summarized view of the problems and difficulties in applying COVID-19 IoT [7, 11].

of a patient's health. Additionally, the data network is incorporated between the equipment and the protocols involved. Figure 9.2 illustrates the summarized vision of the challenges and problems of the pandemic of IoT COVID-19. Also, future data processing and storage work should be aimed at the administrative response. Further research will also explore the methods of making cost-effective adoption requests.

9.9 Conclusion

In answer to COVID-19, IoT offers a robust interrelated network. All these medical devices are internet linked, and in any urgent condition, an alert is automatically sent to the hospital personnel. Unvaccinated instances may be adequately treated with well-connected devices in a distant location. IoT helps in predicting an upcoming situation for this disease by using a statistical-based approach. Researchers, physicians, legislatures, and researchers should create a safer atmosphere for the proper use of this technology to tackle this disease.

References

1. Vaishya, R., Javaid, M., Khan, I. H., & Haleem, A. (2020). Artificial intelligence (AI) applications for COVID-19 pandemic. *Diabetes & Metabolic Syndrome: Clinical Research & Reviews*; 14:337–339. https://doi.org/10.1016/j.dsx.2020.04.012

2. Haleem, A., Javaid, M., & Khan, I. H. (2020). Internet of things (IoT) applications in orthopaedics. *Journal of Clinical Orthopaedics & Trauma; 2019*:S105–S106. https://doi.org/10.1016/j.jcot.2019.07.003

3. Kumar, A., Gupta, P. K., & Srivastava, A. (2020). A review of modern technologies for tackling COVID-19 pandemic. *Diabetes & Metabolic Syndrome: Clinical Research & Reviews;* 14:569–573. https://doi.org/10.1016/j.dsx.2020.05.008

4. Singh, R. P., Javaid M., Kataria, R., Tyagi, M., Haleem, A., & Suman, R. (2020a). Significant applications of virtual reality for COVID-19 pandemic. *Diabetes & Metabolic Syndrome: Clinical Research & Reviews;* 14(4):661–664. https://doi.org/10.1016/j.dsx.2020.05.011

5. Swayamsiddha, S., & Mohanty, C. (2020). Application of cognitive internet of medical things for COVID-19 pandemic. *Diabetes & Metabolic Syndrome: Clinical Research & Reviews;* 14:911–915. https://doi.org/10.1016/j.dsx.2020.06.014

6. Li, B., Yang, D., Wang, X., Tong, L., Zhu, X., Zhong, N., ... & Song, Y. (2020). Chinese experts' consensus on the Internet of Things-aided diagnosis and treatment of coronavirusdisease 2019. *Clinical eHealth; 3*:7–15.

7. Singh, R. P., Javaid, M., Haleem, A., & Suman, R. (2020b). Internet of things (IoT) applications to fight against COVID-19 pandemic. *Diabetes & Metabolic Syndrome: Clinical Research & Reviews;* 14(4):521–524. https://doi.org/10.1016/j.dsx.2020.04.041

8. Ghosh, A., Gupta, R., & Misra, A. (2020). Telemedicine for diabetes care in India during COVID19 pandemic and national lockdown period: guidelines for physicians. *Diabetes & Metabolic Syndrome: Clinical Research & Reviews;* 14(4):273–276. https://doi.org/10.1016/j.dsx.2020.04.001

9. Javaid, M., Haleem, A., Vaishya, R., Bahl, S., Suman, R., & Vaish, A. (2020). Industry 4.0 technologies and their applications in fighting COVID-19 pandemic. *Diabetes & Metabolic Syndrome: Clinical Research & Reviews;* 14:419–422. https://doi.org/10.1016/j.dsx.2020.04.032

10. Nasajpour M., Pouriyeh S., Parizi, R. M., Dorodchi, M., Valero, M., & Arabnia, H. R. (2020). Internet of things for current COVID-19 and future pandemics: An exploratory study. *Journal of Healthcare Informatics Research;* 4:1–40. https://doi.org/10.1007/s41666-020-00080-6

11. Singh, R. P., Javaid, M., Haleem, A., Vaishya, R., & Al, S. (2020c). Internet of medical things (IoMT) for orthopaedic in COVID-19 pandemic: roles, challenges, and applications. *Journal of Clinical Orthopaedics and Trauma;* 11:713–717. https://doi.org/10.1016/j.jcot.2020.05.011

12. Gupta, R., Ghosh, A., Singh, A. K., & Misra, A. (2020). Clinical considerations for patients with diabetes in times of COVID-19 epidemic. *Diabetes & Metabolic Syndrome;* 14(3):211–212. https://doi.org/10.1016/j.dsx.2020.03.002.

13. Wong, T. Y., & Bandello, F. (2020). Academic ophthalmology during and after the COVID-19 pandemic. *Ophthalmology;* 127:51–52.

14. Gopalan, H. S., & Misra, A. (2020). COVID-19 pandemic and challenges for socio-economic issues, healthcare and national programs in India. *Diabetes & Metabolic Syndrome: Clinical Research & Review;* 14(5):757–759. https://doi.org/10.1016/j.dsx.2020.05.041

15. Singh, R. P., Kataria R., & Haq, M. F. U. (2020d). Letter to the editor in response to: COVID-19 pandemic and challenges for socio-economic issues, healthcare and national programs in India (Gopalan and Misra). *Diabetes & Metabolic Syndrome: Clinical Research & Reviews;* 14(5):841–842. https://doi.org/10.1016/j.dsx.2020.06.019

Index